THOMAS DE QUINCEY

RHETORIC IN THE MODERN ERA
_____

Arthur E. Walzer and Edward Schiappa, Editors

The goal of the series "Rhetoric in the Modern Era" is to prompt and sponsor book-length treatments of important rhetorical theorists and of philosophers and literary theorists who make substantial contributions to our understanding of language and rhetoric. In some cases, a book in this series is the first book-length treatment of the figure; in others, a book in the series is the first to examine a philosopher or theorist from the perspective of rhetorical theory.

The intended audience for books in the series is nonspecialists—graduate students coming to the study of a theorist for the first time and professors broadly interested in the rhetorical tradition. The series books are comprehensive introductions—comprehensive in the sense that they provide brief biographies, descriptions of the intellectual milieu, and discussions of the major scholarship on the figure as context for a detailed examination of the figure's contribution to rhetorical theory or history.

We envision these as the first books on their subject, not the last. While books in the series may exceed these modest aims, their focus is on achieving them. A complete list of the books in the series can be found at the end of this volume.

Thomas De Quincey

British Rhetoric's Romantic Turn

LOIS PETERS AGNEW

SOUTHERN ILLINOIS UNIVERSITY PRESS
CARBONDALE AND EDWARDSVILLE

Printed in the United States of America

15 14 13 12   4 3 2 1

Library of Congress Cataloging-in-Publication Data
Agnew, Lois Peters.
Thomas de Quincey : British rhetoric's romantic turn /
Lois Peters Agnew.
    p. cm. — (Rhetoric in the Modern Era)
Includes bibliographical references and index.
ISBN-13: 978-0-8093-3148-2 (pbk. : alk. paper)
ISBN-10: 0-8093-3148-9 (pbk. : alk. paper)
ISBN-13: 978-0-8093-3149-9 (ebook)
ISBN-10: 0-8093-3149-7 (ebook)
1. De Quincey, Thomas, 1785–1859—Criticism and
interpretation. 2. De Quincey, Thomas, 1785–1859—
Knowledge—Literature. 3. Criticism—Great Britain—
History—19th century. I. Title.
PR4537.A74 2012
828'.809—dc23   2012014378

Printed on recycled paper. ♻
The paper used in this publication meets the minimum
requirements of American National Standard for Information Sciences—Permanence of Paper for Printed
Library Materials, ANSI Z39.48-1992. ∞

For Pete, whose belief in me never wavers, whose support for me never falters, and whose remarkable strength inspires me and keeps me going

Contents

Acknowledgments

A number of people have contributed to my work on this project. I first thank the editors of the Rhetoric in the Modern Era series, Arthur E. Walzer and Edward Schiappa, whose interest in the project and excellent suggestions for revision have made this book possible. I also thank Karl Kageff, editor-in-chief at Southern Illinois University Press, for his invaluable support and guidance. I'm also grateful to Barb Martin, SIUP's editing, design, and production manager, who skillfully organized and managed the production process; Wayne Larsen, the SIUP project editor who guided the manuscript through the stages of publication; Mary Lou Kowaleski, whose copyediting was so thoughtful and meticulous; and the entire staff of SIUP for their efficient and insightful work in the various stages of the manuscript's production.

My interest in Thomas De Quincey was first sparked through my study of the history of rhetoric with an extraordinary mentor, Richard Leo Enos, who encouraged me to believe in the importance of questioning gaps in rhetorical history. My recent work on De Quincey has benefited from the support of my colleagues in the Syracuse University Writing Program, particularly Eileen Schell, Collin Brooke, Carol Lipson, and Krista Kennedy, who offered very helpful suggestions in the final phase of revision. Finally, special appreciation goes to my family, Pete, Elizabeth, Peter, Mike, and Luke, for their love, patience, and encouragement.

THOMAS DE QUINCEY

CHAPTER 1

Introduction: Thomas De Quincey's Dialogic Rhetoric

M ost accounts of British rhetorical history end with the 1828 publication of Richard Whately's *Elements of Rhetoric*. The long-standing assumption that Whately speaks the final word about British rhetorical theory has led to gaps in British rhetorical history, as it has obscured other nineteenth-century contributions and implies that British rhetoric simply disappears after the publication of Whately's treatise. More important, this interpretation illustrates a tendency on the part of rhetorical historians to define the field according to a narrow range of principles, limiting our awareness of the complex ways in which people have conceived of rhetoric's potential at various historical moments.

Whately's *Elements* has the advantage of looking like a rhetorical theory; it can easily be recognized as contributing to a long line of treatises that prepare people for effective participation in public life. Other nineteenth-century British writings about language's capacity to foster meaningful public and private interactions might appear less relevant to the immediate, practical aims found in rhetorical treatises grounded, as Whately's is, in the Aristotelian tradition. The importance of these less-traditional texts to rhetorical history stems from the very fact of their departure from what we might expect a rhetorical theory to look like. These varied nineteenth-century approaches illustrate rhetoric's dynamic capacity to respond to unique cultural circumstances in ways that differ markedly from what has come to be seen as the status quo. Nineteenth-century British rhetoric has a history beyond Whately; the recognition of this fact underscores rhetoric's resilience, expands the parameters we use in defining rhetoric, points to specific directions theorists take in responding to changing technologies and cultural perspectives, and reveals significant trends that emerge in rhetoric's transition to the modern era.

These benefits are particularly evident in a study of Thomas De Quincey's rhetorical theory. De Quincey (1785–1859) is best known for his writings about opium use, but his remarkable literary production includes essays on a wide range of topics, including rhetoric, language, and style. De Quincey's view of rhetoric has received scattered interest among rhetoric scholars from his own day to the present, but it merits further attention, both in its own right and as a significant benchmark in the transition from eighteenth-century belletristic rhetorics to British rhetoric's nineteenth-century Romantic turn.

In *Outward, Visible Propriety: Stoic Philosophy and Eighteenth-Century British Rhetorics*, I argue that eighteenth-century rhetorical theorists drew heavily on Stoic philosophy in an effort to cling to the classical ideal of sensus communis during a period of intense social change. The final chapter of that book explores ways in which nineteenth-century writers such as De Quincey, Thomas Carlyle, Matthew Arnold, Vernon Lee, Walter Pater, and Oscar Wilde pursue notions of language that depart more substantially from the civic goals that had sustained much of rhetoric's development in earlier eras. While the ideas developed by these nineteenth-century writers are clearly distinct from rhetorical theories grounded in classical principles of persuasion and the idealistic goal of sensus communis, they, nevertheless, sustain rhetoric's development through their interest in the public and private functions of language. They also demonstrate rhetoric's resiliency through devising notions of language that both build on and transform earlier theories in ways that respond to the conditions of their age. De Quincey is particularly important among those writers who contribute to British rhetoric's transformation in the nineteenth century. De Quincey's ideas about rhetoric offer an appropriate starting point for filling previous gaps in traditional accounts of nineteenth-century British rhetorical history, as his perspective on language and public life is grounded in classical rhetorical traditions, yet radically distinct from those traditions in ways that reflect his attention to the cultural circumstances in which he finds himself.

The transitional character of De Quincey's rhetorical theory, therefore, merits attention not only as an intriguing conception of rhetoric but also because it illuminates the broader transformation that takes place in British rhetorical theories during the nineteenth century. De Quincey offers a nineteenth-century view of rhetoric that differs significantly from Whately's more traditional treatise, which signals several strains of development in nineteenth-century British rhetoric. Moreover, De Quincey's rhetoric exemplifies the dynamic relationship between rhetoric and its cultural surroundings and offers insight into key principles and concerns that alter rhetoric's development during the latter decades of the nineteenth century.

There is no question that rhetoric undergoes a change in nineteenth-century Britain. A general distrust of the rhetorical tradition is reflected in the work of numerous nineteenth-century writers who appear to endorse Carlyle's 1834 pronouncement that the times require that "one leaves the pasteboard coulisses, and three Unities, and Blair[']s Lectures, quite behind; and feels only that there is *nothing sacred*, then, but the *Speech of Man* to believing Men!" ("Letter" 1:22–23). Various prominent writers share Carlyle's view that the traditional structures surrounding rhetorical training and practice have contributed to society's apparent decline. This perspective illustrates a change in rhetoric's fortunes during the nineteenth century, but it by no means indicates that rhetoric disappeared without a trace. Winifred Bryan Horner and Kerri Morris Barton counter the view that rhetoric began a "decline" in the eighteenth century by noting that rhetoric's development requires an awareness that terminology changes with rhetorical principles: "Rhetoric survived under other names, and as the basic concepts changed focus the terminology changed as well. The actual effects of these changes were far-reaching as rhetoric spread over a number of disciplines in the nineteenth- and twentieth-century academic communities" (114). Horner and Barton note that new formulations of rhetoric emerge through the eighteenth-century interest in literature and psychology, an emphasis on vernacular education aimed at the development of practical skills, and "the shift from rhetoric's emphasis on speakers and the generative aspects of texts to an emphasis on readers and their interpretations of texts" (115). Nineteenth-century changes in rhetoric are also shaped in part by the ready access to print, which disseminated ideas with greater diffusion across a broader spectrum of society. As Jason Camlot argues, rhetoric in the nineteenth century "does not so much disappear as it becomes scattered piecemeal in the essays of the burgeoning nineteenth-century literary magazines and reviews" (6). The nineteenth century sustains, develops, and complicates eighteenth-century trends to extend rhetoric's sphere into widely ranging disciplines and to complicate rhetoric's role in the production and consumption of different textual genres.

An awareness of nineteenth-century changes in rhetoric's orientation and in the vocabulary that surrounds rhetorical production is particularly useful in tracking the rhetorical strains in nineteenth-century British writings influenced by Romantic thought, such as De Quincey's. In spite of De Quincey's corpus including essays titled "Rhetoric" and "Style," his ties to Romanticism may in part account for the fact that he has received relatively little attention from rhetoric scholars. In their introduction to *Rhetorical Traditions and British Romantic Literature*, Don H. Bialostosky and Lawrence D. Needham describe the tendency among scholars to dismiss Romanticism entirely from rhetorical history: "That rhetoric declined as Romanticism rose is the commonest of commonplaces, a story seemingly agreed to by all parties" (introduction 1). Rex Veeder argues that the turn toward Romanticism did not do away with rhetoric altogether but altered the vocabulary surrounding rhetorical practice in ways that function on a continuum with the eighteenth century: "The British Romantics were interested in the same rhetorical issues as Hugh Blair, George Campbell, and Richard Whately, but the terms they used varied greatly. . . . The British Romantics were as much a part of the 18th as the 19th century, and the tendency, perhaps as a result of the Ramist debate, to call rhetoric by many names lasted throughout both centuries" ("Expressive Rhetoric" 100). The search for an understanding of rhetoric's presence in the midst of its dispersal through the use of "many names" calls for an investigation of what types of cultural and philosophical changes contributed to rhetoric's apparent decline in the nineteenth century, how rhetorical theories and practices adapted to those changes, and how rhetoric's evolution in the nineteenth century deviates from scholarly assumptions about rhetoric in ways that explain why so many accounts of British rhetorical history end with Whately. De Quincey's fusion of rhetoric and Romanticism provides an important site for considering these questions.

De Quincey's perception that society was going through unprecedented and to some extent unwelcome change was an idea common among British intellectuals in the early decades of the nineteenth century. The changes that were of concern to De Quincey can generally be identified as part of the shift from an agrarian to an industrial society, a change whose consequences were becoming increasingly evident as De Quincey began his adult years. John W. Osborne's depiction of a "silent revolution" in nineteenth-century Britain focuses on the significant social changes brought about through the rapid economic expansion that took place in Britain during the early decades. Osborne identifies the decade of the 1780s as a turning point that signals the beginning of society's rapid transformation to mass markets and mechanized efficiency, a change facilitated through the rise in manufacturing and improved methods of travel (21–31). Osborne describes these measures as expanding the parameters for social exchange and diminishing the appreciation for individual craftsmanship, a change that had significant consequences for workers and for a society increasingly oriented toward mass production. He argues that "among the important changes of the Silent Revolution were the regularization of work and the discipline of labor" (31), adding that as the worker was "regulated by factory rules and deprived of his individuality, he was more and more at the mercy of impersonal economic forces beyond his control" (39). The shift away from craftsmanship had immediate and potentially troubling implications for the long-standing interest in taste, which Donald Pilcher describes as responding to "materials whose final appearance was no longer decided by the individual touch of a craftsman, but by the standardising stamp of the machine" (170). Bialostosky and Needham emphasize the importance of this phenomenon during the rise of Romanticism, as the increase in print production put new pressures on writers who were accountable to a wider public: "New exigencies demanding a full arsenal of verbal resources was the emergence of a new scene of writing that followed the decline of patronage and the rise of market forces as factors determining a writer's career" (introduction 7). Although Pilcher goes on to say that many people in the nineteenth century might have found themselves able to believe that "the machine was a heaven-sent answer to the demand for taste" (170), many others were undoubtedly concerned that machines had intruded into a domain that had for centuries been defined as part of a natural human ability to judge beauty and develop successful interpersonal communication. (For a more complete discussion of the significance of taste in eighteenth- and nineteenth-century theories of language and rhetoric, see Agnew, "Civic Function"; Cohen; Crowley; Ferreira-Buckley and Halloran; Johnson; Ulman.)

Osborne notes that the shift away from individuality and personal relationships had particular consequences for political oratory: "Slowly the collective ego of the House of Commons began to alter. The ability to inspire affection, which had enabled Charles James Fox to possess great power, became less important and the same was true of oratorical skill. The younger Pitt, whose reserve and hauteur were bywords to his contemporaries, would have seemed hypersensitive in a less sentimental age and his renowned oratory theatrical to men accustomed to a brisker pace in legislative affairs" (87). Such changes in the way people conceived of communication and social relations support T. S. Ashton's view that the period typically described as "the Industrial Revolution" must be understood to contain a revolution that was "not merely 'industrial,' but also social and intellectual" (64). Changing attitudes toward political discourse undoubtedly played a role in the widespread assumption that the parameters for rhetorical production must be revised.

It is not surprising that this social and intellectual change included a struggle over the reading practices of an increasingly literate public. Richard Altick explains that the alteration in the economy created by industrialism created "a sharpening of class consciousness" that included, on one hand, expanded opportunities for many people to achieve social advancement and political rights and, on the other hand, efforts on the part of those who had historically been the guardians of social capital to maintain "their own position against the newly arrived" (85). Altick identifies expanded opportunities for literacy as a central issue that shapes contested claims about the formation of national values: "Once they conceded it was impossible to prevent the lower ranks from reading, they embarked on a long campaign to insure that through the press the masses of people would be induced to help preserve the status quo and bulwark the security and prosperity of the particular sort of national life that they, its upper- and middle-class rulers, cherished" (85). Thus, nineteenth-century change represented both opportunity and struggle.

Although numerous historical accounts support the interpretation of the alteration in nineteenth-century British society as radical, unique, and unprecedented, it is at the same time important to qualify this view. In *British Society, 1680–1880: Dynamism, Containment, and Change*, Richard Price argues that the common view of the nineteenth century as the threshold to modernity needs to be adjusted in order to acknowledge continuity existing across British society from the late seventeenth century through the latter part of the nineteenth century. However, Price acknowledges that the radical transformation of nineteenth-century British society is an image historians acquired from texts written during that period: "The idea that the early nineteenth century was the moment of modernity, the turning point from the 'old' world to the 'new' is not an invention of historians. It was an invention of the early Victorian intelligentsia. The notion of transition was a commonplace among the early and mid-Victorian intellectual elite" (4). Robin Gilmour echoes this view, noting that the intelligentsia's sense of a society in flux meant that "more than any previous generation the people we call Victorians were driven to find models of social harmony and personal conduct by means of which they could understand, control, and develop their rapidly changing world" (20). Price makes a compelling argument for the importance of recognizing the contemporary foundations of early Victorian concerns in a way that challenges the wholesale appropriation of this interpretation into historical accounts of the period; however, he, Gilmour, and others acknowledge that people experiencing life in nineteenth-century Britain were searching for a sense of stability in what they saw as unprecedented shifts in their social landscape. Carlyle's lament over a society that has "grown mechanical in head and in heart" ("Signs" 63) is one shared by many nineteenth-century writers who feared that a fascination with manufacturing and machines had brought on a decline in their society's intellectual strength.

Their sense of the detrimental effects of social change inspired literary conservatives such as William Wordsworth, Osborne notes, to fight for a return to the social relationships that they perceived that commercial interests threatened. The emergence of this priority defines Romanticism and accounts for contemporary writings that emphasize the damaging effects of industrial society. Although he acknowledges that the effects of industrialism had begun to take effect long before the Romantic era, Karl Kroeber argues that it was in that period that people became fully aware that society was undergoing significant change: "In the Romantic period consciousness of the 'mass' culture associated with industrialism . . . began to develop" (2). Raymond Williams describes Romantic artists as responding to this "mass culture" by defining their role "as bearers of the creative imagination" capable of inspiring a vision of deeper human values than those advanced by the commercial interests that dominated their society: "The emphasis on a general common humanity was evidently necessary in a period in which a new kind of society was coming to think of man as merely a specialized instrument of production. The emphasis on love and relationship was necessary not only within the immediate suffering but against the aggressive individualism and the primarily economic relationships which the new society embodied" (42). This emphasis on the immediacy of social relationships, strengthened through the intensive imaginative activity of the creative individual, provides a counter not only to the changes perceived to be part of an increasing shift toward mechanical production in the nineteenth century but also to the emphasis on system and order that had characterized traditional eighteenth-century rhetorical theories.

This concern must be understood as a dominant feature of De Quincey's thinking about rhetoric and language, as De Quincey adds his own critique of "the elegant but desultory Blair" ("Style" 192) to Carlyle's negative assessment of the systematic approach to rhetoric that Blair's lectures typified ("Letter" 1: 22). De Quincey's rhetoric emerges in an intellectual environment Wordsworth shaped with sharp criticism of the damage that the conditions of industrial society had brought about:

> For a multitude of causes, unknown to former times, are now acting with a combined force to blunt the discriminating powers of the mind and, unfitting it for all voluntary exertion, to reduce it to a state of almost savage torpor. The most effective of these causes are the great national events which are daily taking place, and the increasing accumulation of men in cities, where the uniformity of their occupations produces a craving for extraordinary incident, which the rapid communication of intelligence hourly gratifies. To this tendency of life and manners the literature and theatrical exhibitions of the country have conformed themselves. (Preface 64)

De Quincey shares Wordsworth's conviction that an "almost savage torpor" has overtaken British culture; the key to De Quincey's Romantic vision of rhetoric lies in his persistent representation of the creative imagination as a counter to the restrictive drive for efficiency found in industrial society.

Yet, Price's reminder that the alteration in nineteenth-century society was neither absolute nor abrupt must also be taken into account in studying De Quincey's work. Price's statement that during the early decades of the nineteenth century, "the pressures for change were enclosed within estab-lished and familiar boundaries and did not disrupt the fields of engagement in society" (12) provides an important framework for grasping the gradual transformation of nineteenth-century British ideas, a characteristic that applies to Romantic thought. In her analysis of Wordsworth, Theresa M. Kelley challenges characterizations of Romantic invention as unequivocally based in notions of genius and originality: "Wordsworth's poetic practice, said to be exemplary (for good or ill) of Romantic poetics, is complexly bound to the exigencies of traditional rhetoric even as it wrenches away from specific tropes or devices" (124). De Quincey participates in what Kelley describes as a feature of the writing of Wordsworth and other Romantics, "a pattern of citation that is cumulative, historical, and social" (124), a pat-tern evident in De Quincey's determination to invoke connections between his approach to rhetoric and Aristotle's more systematic search for "the available means of persuasion" (Aristotle 1:ii). De Quincey's essays offer an important resource for locating those principles of rhetoric that are sustained from earlier generations, as well as ideas concerning communication and society that are altered in response to changing social conditions and new venues for publication.

De Quincey's development of a new vision of rhetoric thus emerges from his unique position in the transition from one era to another—and from a character uniquely attentive to the implications of that transition. De Quincey biographer Edward Sackville-West is keenly aware of De Quincey's location at a historical crossroads, as he demonstrates in his poetic description of the period when De Quincey takes up residence in London in 1802:

> London, which seemed to Thomas a nightmare and a portent, was now, in the year 1802, at a transition stage of its development. It had not yet acquired all the driving ambition and turbid hurry of the industrial age, which was beginning, nor had the dour fog of Victorian England yet settled down upon it. On the other hand, the spacious ease and dignity of the eighteenth century were fast disappearing, and in its disintegration incongruous fragments of both centuries lived side by side, all but unconscious of each other. (55–56)

De Quincey's awareness of his position alongside "incongruous fragments of both centuries" and his immersion in a historical "transition stage" in part accounts for his development of a theory that can be said above all to signal a rhetorical transition stage. This theory can be seen as intricately connected with the complex character of De Quincey, whom Sackville-West describes as "[i]n many small ways a man of the eighteenth century" (190) but whose emphasis on the subjective exploration of multiple possibilities decidedly moves beyond the boundaries of eighteenth-century rhetorical theories.

The task of defining the guiding principles of De Quincey's contribution to rhetoric's nineteenth-century transition involves challenges that emerge in discussing any writer who is associated with Romanticism. In the influential article "On the Discrimination of Romanticisms," Arthur O. Lovejoy describes the difficulty of establishing a clear sense of the terms connected with Romanticism: "The word 'romantic' has come to mean so many things that, by itself, it means nothing. It has ceased to perform the function of a verbal sign" (6). As a solution to this problem, Lovejoy proposes to confront the multiplicity of Romanticism directly, as he argues that "any study of the subject should begin with a recognition of a *prima-facie* plurality of Romanticisms, of possibly quite distinct thought-complexes, a number of which may appear in one country" (8). Certainly, the need to recognize the plurality of Romanticisms is evident in any study of De Quincey, whose intellectual formation was substantially influenced by Wordsworth and Samuel Taylor Coleridge but who supplemented those formative influences with a wide array of experiences and reading material, including the works of German metaphysicians and an intimate knowledge of classical texts, in developing ideas that reflect his particular version of a Romantic rhetoric.

One of the central Romantic values that guides De Quincey's thought is the unrestricted pursuit of intellectual potential. For De Quincey, such an endeavor should emphasize self-discovery above self-expression, a process that is framed as an intellectual and social endeavor. In this respect, De Quincey deviates from the focus on nature characteristic of many of his peers; although De Quincey shared Wordsworth's appreciation for the Lake District and spent much of his life there, biographer Robert Morrison describes De Quincey as "a different kind of Laker. . . . As absorbed as he was by Wordsworth's poetry, he did not show much of an interest himself in waterfalls or sheepfolds or sunrises or daffodils. Instead, his interest in the area revolved around its people, its history, and its customs" (*English Opium-Eater* 153). De Quincey's rhetoric also diverges from Wordsworth's famous definition of poetry as "the spontaneous overflow of powerful feelings" (62); De Quincey's rhetoric is not a forum for an outpouring of emotive expression but is, instead, the means for individuals to acquire new insights through a detached investigation of multiple perspectives. For De Quincey, self-discovery is defined in terms that correspond to German Romanticism as guided by Johann Christoph Friedrich von Schiller, whose writings De Quincey appreciated and translated for several British periodicals. Lovejoy explains that, for Schiller, "'harmony with nature,' in any sense which implied an opposition to 'culture,' to 'art,' to reflection and self-conscious effort, was neither possible nor desirable for the modern man or the modern artist" (15). Instead, Schiller strikingly parallels De Quincey in arguing that art "should seek first fulness of content, should have for its program the adequate expression of the entire range of human experience and the entire reach of the human imagination. For man, the artificial, Friedrich Schlegel observed, *is* 'natural'" (15; original emphasis). De Quincey, too, pursues "the entire range of human experience and the entire reach of the human imagination" through language, a pursuit that acknowledges artificiality as an element of rhetorical practice. Like Coleridge, who holds that poetry "is opposed to works of science, by proposing for its *immediate* object pleasure, not truth" (172; original emphasis), De Quincey maintains that rhetoric's pursuit is the pleasurable investigation of possibility, which necessarily sets aside the search for certain truth. At the heart of De Quincey's Romanticism is the conviction that a playful artifice plays an important role in the full exploration of humanity's creative intellectual potential.

This conviction naturally corresponds to De Quincey's strong commitment to exploring possibilities, an objective he enacts so fully that in both his personal life and writings, he underscores the paradoxical complexity that surrounds Romantic ideals. While De Quincey resisted the system and order that he perceived as intellectually limiting the open investigation of multiple perspectives, he was an ardent Tory whose political views were typically conservative, nationalistic, and imperialistic. In describing De Quincey's interest in secret societies, Morrison notes that this preoccupation "throws into relief the two powerful and often competing interests at the core of his intellect: an Enlightenment-based investment in classicism, and an anti-Enlightenment enthusiasm for mystery, mystification, and disorder" (*English Opium-Eater* 31). The tension underlying De Quincey's thought helps to account for his pattern of being drawn toward views that are seemingly incompatible with each other. Morrison describes the pull of opposing ideologies in suggesting that De Quincey might have been attracted by the radical politics of his wife Margaret's family, even as he continually tried to persuade them of his own Tory views, "for despite his own rebelliousness, De Quincey was a determined advocate of the status quo" (*English Opium-Eater* 166–67). In politics, along with broader intellectual pursuits, De Quincey's commitment to the rhetorical investigation of multiple perspectives accounts for his own tendency to entertain opposing political positions. Morrison also explains that De Quincey's ability to write for periodicals with differing political views related to his own disposition to see multiple sides of the question: "Though sometimes tarred as a furious right-winger, De Quincey's sympathies extended to both sides of the political spectrum" (*English Opium-Eater* 285). De Quincey's practice of the open inquiry he advocates for rhetoric is evident in his political flexibility, described in an 1861 *Quarterly Review* essay: "He was ready to challenge all comers, to investigate all problems, to hold every truth up to the light" (qtd. in *English Opium-Eater* 285). Thus, De Quincey theorizes and practices a Romantic rhetoric that resists certainty and closure, uniquely blending controversy and conservatism, freedom and restraint.

Paradox also permeates De Quincey's relationship with technology. While he strongly shares Wordsworth's suspicion of "the rapid communication of intelligence" brought about by the mass distribution of print, he, along with other nineteenth-century intellectuals, was unable to escape the effects of the machine age on his own artistic production. His Romantic vision of the creative power of the individual reflects the particular tension inherent in his position as a prose writer dependent on the income he received from the periodical press. Lee Erickson describes "the industrial-ization of publishing" (188) in the nineteenth century as a factor that "led many authors to feel alienated both from their own work and also from the common reader" (189). Erickson highlights the inherent tensions many periodical writers experienced: "The great irony of the transformation in the conditions of literary production was that authors felt their influence upon society diminished even as they saw that the possibilities for it were enormously expanded—hence their ambivalence toward the publishing marketplace where a commodity value was placed on their work" (189). De Quincey's writings reveal the ambivalence Erickson describes; his ar-ticulation of the power of language available through the creative enterprise of the individual stands in sharp contrast with his own position as a writer for periodicals who felt deeply the burden of writing for a mass audience. Camlot writes that "[w]hat is most at odds in De Quincey . . . is his romantic understanding of solitude, which he employs against the alienating pros-pect of a large periodicals audience, and the practical solitude and isolation imposed by a developing print culture upon a professional writer" (86). The opposition Camlot describes is both a defining feature of De Quincey's work and a component of a rhetorical theory that responds directly to the unique cultural conditions that surrounded De Quincey in the early decades of the nineteenth century.

A key principle that De Quincey carries forward from previous itera-tions of British rhetorical theories is the significant role of language in the formation of social and individual identity. However, De Quincey's cultural location leads him to resist the unifying tendencies that had characterized many earlier rhetorical strains. This resistance is a particular example of De Quincey's affiliation with Romantic thought, which Kroeber describes as guided by a focus on "[i]magination, the capacity to unify diverse realities and seemingly incompatible experiences in order to represent the paradoxical actuality of life concealed within conventional orderings of it" (17–18). For De Quincey, the paradoxical potential of the imagination is best realized through a vision of rhetoric that is dialogic.

In *The Dialogic Imagination*, Mikhail M. Bakhtin identifies the move to a dialogic perspective in the novel as "an enormous revolution in the cre-ative consciousness of man" (38) grounded in "personal experience and free creative imagination" (39). For Bakhtin, the decline of the epic and the rise of the novel signals an opportunity to discover the potential of "a dialogue between points of view" (76). Just as Bakhtin acknowledges the rhetorical dimensions available through the novel (268), De Quincey's rhetoric can be seen as participating in the dialogic form exemplified in the novel. He shares Bakhtin's recognition that "the living utterance . . . cannot fail to become an active participant in social dialogue" (Bakhtin 276), as he produces a vision of rhetoric constituted by "internal dialogism of the word" (Bakhtin 282) in which the speaker/writer interacts constantly with listeners who hold differing points of view and imaginatively integrates those perspectives as a feature of the expansive rhetorical process.

The uniqueness of De Quincey's dialogic approach begins to become apparent through a comparison of De Quincey with Whately. De Quincey himself points toward this comparison in presenting many of his ideas about rhetoric in a review essay of Whately's *Elements of Rhetoric* titled "Rhetoric," published in an 1828 issue of *Blackwood's* magazine. Although De Quincey's essay lacks the consistent engagement with Whately's book that readers might expect to see in a review, his articulation of his own principles of rhetoric in that essay establishes a definite contrast from those Whately advances in his treatise. Although both Whately and De Quincey develop versions of rhetoric that respond to concerns specific to their own cultural surroundings, Whately's theory is more squarely aligned with traditional assumptions about rhetoric's role in civic life. He positions himself in the preface as offering a system that might guide those who need instruction in rhetorical practices (*Elements* 7), and that system covers territory that is familiar to rhetoric scholars. In keeping with the pattern found in the ancient treatises of Aristotle and Quintilian, Whately begins with a thorough survey of varying definitions of rhetoric, concluding that his own work will "treat of 'Argumentative Composition,' *generally* and *exclusively*; considering Rhetoric (in conformity with the very just and philosophical view of Aristotle) as an offshoot from Logic" (21; original emphasis). In addition to endorsing Aristotle's interpretation of rhetoric's relationship to logic, Whately praises Aristotle as "the best of the systematic writers on Rhetoric" (24). The remainder of Whately's treatise illustrates his adaptation of Aristotle's systematic approach for an early-nineteenth-century context, as Whately offers his version of the classical canons of invention, arrangement, style, and delivery in methodically labeled sections, chapters, and paragraphs. Although his treatise offers distinct ideas about rhetoric that emerge from his engagement with nineteenth-century concerns, particularly in his attention to written composition, Whately's construction of a system that applies logical reasoning processes to specific public rhetorical contexts demonstrates important and obvious connections to Aristotle's rhetoric.

De Quincey also insists upon his own connection to Aristotle's view of rhetoric, but his basis for claiming such a connection is more elusive. Unlike Whately's *Elements*, De Quincey's essay on rhetoric has no structural similarities to Aristotle's *Rhetoric*; he makes no effort to provide a systematic treatment of the rhetorical canons, and he eschews any concern with the rhetorical genres or the civic settings in which rhetoric might be found. Instead, De Quincey bases his affiliation with Aristotle on what he conceives as their shared focus on probability; he maintains that Aristotle "threw the whole stress upon finding such arguments for any given thesis as, without positively proving or disproving it, should give it a colourable support" ("Rhetoric" 85–86). While he fails to engage directly with topical invention, De Quincey cites Aristotle's use of the topics as evidence of his interest in lines of reasoning that are aimed not at determining truth but at offering plausibility, which he describes as the "real governing law of Aristotle's procedure" (86). In this way, De Quincey claims that his view of rhetoric invokes the true spirit of Aristotle's rhetoric, even as he develops ideas that radically depart from Aristotle's famous presentation of a systematic theory grounded in the goal of reaching collective judgment about civic affairs. His argument thus illustrates the dialogic method he advocates, as he insists upon claiming that the model for his very untraditional rhetoric is one of the most traditional rhetorical treatises, in the process revealing his own proficiency at engaging with multiple interpretive possibilities in order to encourage the reader's consideration of a plausible point of view that had not been available previously, offering not definitive proof of that position but "colourable support" for considering its merits.

De Quincey's discussion of rhetoric prompted a lengthy footnote by David Masson, the editor of his collected works, which depicts De Quincey's interpretation of Aristotle as entirely mistaken. What Masson fails to acknowledge is De Quincey's effort to explore a possible reading of Aristotle rather than presenting a certain or true statement of Aristotle's theory, an approach that demonstrates the rhetorical method he advocates. In place of the traditional goal of resolution, De Quincey conceives of rhetoric as a dialogical process that achieves its meaning primarily from the intellectual activity involved in the process of investigating varied alternatives. He identifies rhetoric's domain as those situations in which opposing alternatives may be considered legitimate, "*cases where there is pro and con . . . affirmative and negative are both true*" ("Rhetoric" 91; original emphasis). The rhetorician enters into such situations and "exhibits his art by giving an impulse to one side, and by withdrawing the mind so steadily from all thoughts or images which support the other as to leave it practically under the possession of a one-sided estimate" (91). In De Quincey's mind, such an artistic exhibition holds important intellectual value but need not be connected to practical decision making. He insists that "where conviction begins, the field of Rhetoric ends" (82), a definite expression of his emphasis on preserving rhetoric's capacity to explore multiple possibilities. His claim for the leisurely exploration of possibility constitutes an emphatic response to what he considers to be changes detrimental to the social and intellectual life of nineteenth-century society. De Quincey's dialogic rhetoric enacts his romantic vision of an expansive intellectual space that can counter the demands for practicality and efficiency that had become a feature of nineteenth-century British discourse and public life.

Such a vision corresponds closely to what Bialostosky describes as central to a Wordsworthian tradition that is both dialogic and rhetorical in nature: "[T]he tradition I advocate thrives in a field of contestation and requires the co-presence of forcefully articulated alternatives to make its own force felt. It is characterized, in fact, precisely by the preservation and highlighting of alternative voices that the unifying and idealizing Coleridgean tradition 'dissolves and dissipates'" (*Wordsworth* 39). Yet, although De Quincey develops a conception of rhetoric that certainly shares Wordsworth's appreciation for the exploration of multiple possibilities, calls for the "co-presence of forcefully articulated alternatives," and insists upon a thorough engagement with alternative perspectives, his version of rhetoric's dialogic potential has several important differences from the features of the Wordsworthian tradition that Bialostosky identifies. It is significant that De Quincey cites Aristotle and therefore aligns himself with "the Aristotelian disciplinary system" (Bialostosky, *Wordsworth* 39), even as he argues for a conception of rhetoric that undermines the orderly system Aristotle had postulated. He also counters Wordsworth's use of "alternative voices" (Bialostosky, *Wordsworth* 39) created through his effort "to adopt the very language of men" (Wordsworth 65), offering instead rhetoric's capacity to illuminate reality through a strategic artificiality. Thus, De Quincey participates in what Bialostosky describes as the resistance to "disciplinary boundaries" exemplified by Gorgias and Wordsworth, including "a common perspective in which poetry, rhetoric, history, philosophy, and science are being freshly distinguished as related kinds of discourse dependent upon common verbal powers and related pleasurable interests" (*Wordsworth* 40). However, De Quincey at the same time connects himself with the disciplinary tradition that his work ostensibly resists and eschews any claim that the creative enterprise he advocates can be seen as natural and authentic. These differences exemplify De Quincey's thoroughgoing enactment of the dialogic potential he sees in rhetoric as he persistently embraces the paradoxes that pervade his own theories.

The next chapter argues that De Quincey's notion that rhetoric is grounded in the intellectual activity of the individual makes knowledge of his own life and the key events that shaped his intellectual formation particularly important in understanding his rhetorical theory. His emphasis on rhetorical subjectivity is evident in his literary corpus; two volumes of Masson's fourteen-volume collection of De Quincey's writings consist primarily of autobiographical essays, while a third contains his most famous work, *Confessions of an English Opium-Eater.* Julianne Smith argues that De Quincey's life and writing are intricately linked, a relationship that ultimately shapes his approach to rhetoric: "De Quincey's discontinuous approach to writing reflected the erratic habits and behaviors found in other parts of his life as well. . . . His erratic lifestyle, his arrogance, and his writing habits were not conducive to a systematic approach to the topic of rhetoric such as we have come to expect from the classical tradition" (45). Smith also maintains that the disjunction between De Quincey and the classical tradition, including his emphasis on rhetorical creativity, is firmly grounded in De Quincey's own material circumstances, including the financial need that continually plagued him: "De Quincey is not as interested, for example, in Quintilian's concept of the rhetor as a 'good man speaking well' as he is in alternately keeping his debtors at bay and practicing a new kind of eloquence—an eloquence that is, perhaps, difficult to define but that grows out of a vital internal creative energy based on both intellect and experience" (45). Smith concludes that "a compelling connection exists between De Quincey's personal writing practices, his ethos, and his notions about rhetoric" (46).

Such a connection can be seen as part of De Quincey's response to the cultural context within which he operates. Gilmour notes that autobiography was an important element of the Victorian response to social instability: "Holding the world together within, finding a coherence in the self which would at the same time impose some meaning and coherence on a rapidly changing world outside: this involved searching for a logic in one's own memories, which is the task of autobiography" (27). However, the stability and coherence De Quincey seeks through autobiography must be understood as distinct from the dull insistence upon certainty he associates with a society driven by machines and a market economy. De Quincey's rhetoric is defined by an immersion in possibility that he perceives as fundamental to the development of intellectual power. De Quincey shares Carlyle's sense that the remedy for a society "mechanical in head and in heart" lies in language that fosters the intellectual empowerment of individuals rather than clear language that facilitates smooth business transactions.

De Quincey's determination to connect rhetoric to his own subjectivity, particularly in light of the controversies surrounding elements of his personal life, may in part account for some of the strongly negative assessments of De Quincey's work. Rene Wellek characterizes De Quincey as "a strictly 'occasional' writer who wrote, over a long period of years, miscellaneous articles with specific purposes, in special moods, with little unity beyond that of his temperament and style" (249). While Wellek, like Smith, accurately captures the personal exigencies surrounding De Quincey's literary production, his argument fails to account for the fact that De Quincey's conception of rhetoric provides interesting insight into the significance of "unity . . . of temperament and style" as an end in itself—and helps to illuminate the rationale for a nineteenth-century turn toward a rhetoric grounded in discovery rather than finality.

Additional attention to De Quincey's interest in rhetoric underscores his emphasis on intellectual exploration as an ultimate value that resists what he perceives to be the stultifying environment of a society dominated by commercial concerns—and his attempt to embody that dialogical process in his writings. To ground rhetoric's potential in the individual's subjective investigation of the world inevitably allows for changes in mood, temperament, and motivation guided by the writer's internal state, which poses a challenge to a tradition largely based on rhetoric's capacity to promote clear communication between rhetor and audience. De Quincey's writings suggest interesting possibilities that come about as rhetoric moves outside the boundaries of clarity and precision, but they also illustrate the challenges that emerge when rhetoric is removed from its traditional concern with audience and context. The tensions evident in a conception of rhetoric as a free and imaginative enterprise transcending the ordinary conduct of human affairs are mirrored in De Quincey's own biography, which illustrates the difficulties encountered by the individual whose rhetorical vision cannot be easily reconciled with the practical demands of everyday life.

CHAPTER 2

De Quincey's Life

De Quincey's rhetoric emphasizes subjectivity, an orientation that is reflected in his own literary corpus, which focuses extensively on the events of his life and his complex interpretation of those events. As discussed in the previous chapter, De Quincey conceives of rhetoric as an intensive, subjective exploration of multiple possibilities, a dialogic activity carried out by the imaginative individual who develops intellectual power through engaging with a range of alternatives ("Rhetoric" 91). For De Quincey, the rhetorician's ability to share his or her perspective on the world through vivid and disciplined language use is an essential element in the artistic endeavor of providing "colourable support" ("Rhetoric" 86) for positions that cannot be definitively proved. De Quincey's life story illustrates the unique balance between tradition and innovation that characterizes his theories of rhetoric and language; De Quincey's personal history illustrates the Romantic effort to "unify diverse realities and seemingly incompatible experiences in order to represent the paradoxical actuality of life concealed within conventional orderings of it" (Kroeber 17–18). It also reveals his persistent effort to explore alternative possibilities and to enact those possibilities through his writing.

There is abundant evidence that De Quincey considered attention to multiple alternatives not only a central theoretical touchstone for rhetoric but also a key feature of his own personality. He significantly identifies this quality as one lacking in his friend Wordsworth in a section of the controversial essay titled "Gradual Estrangement from Wordsworth." In one section of that essay, he analyzes Wordsworth's character through his reading of German philosophy, explaining that he acquired a new understanding of Wordsworth from the concept of "*einseitigkeit, or one-sidedness,* as a peculiarity not unfrequently besetting the strongest minds" ("Gradual Estrangement" 204). De Quincey's assessment that Wordsworth was "*einseitig* in extremity" (204) not only provides a justification for his critique of Wordsworth but also underscores his own preference for thoroughly considering multiple dimensions of a subject and acknowledging the potential validity that can be seen in many positions, a commitment that is a guiding principle in his rhetorical theory.

De Quincey was born in Manchester on August 15, 1785, to Elizabeth Penson Quincey and Thomas Quincey, a prosperous linen merchant. Key components of De Quincey's family history anticipate his appreciation for the value of considering multiple perspectives. Even something as seemingly straightforward as the family name proved to be open to change and interpretation on the part of different family members, as De Quincey's daughter Florence Baird Smith explains in an 1890 letter to the editor of *Macmillan's* magazine:

> [A]t the time my Grandfather began business . . . he dropped the de in the belief that the suggestion of a foreign origin was a disadvantage in a commercial career at that time. When the family withdrew from the business, the de was resumed, and used by the whole family. In the course of time the increasing stringency of the mother's evangelical views induced her to drop it again, as a worldly vanity, her three sons who grew to manhood did not adopt these views and continued the de. ("[Correspondence between Mrs. Bairdsmith and the editor]")

Thus, De Quincey began his life with an awareness that even apparently fixed facts of family identity may be altered in order to reflect family members' varied priorities and values. His awareness of this is evident in *Confessions of an English Opium-Eater*, in which he offers a footnote concerning the family name early in the text (286), which in turn refers the reader to a characteristically lengthy excursus on that topic in an appendix (457–59). De Quincey's whimsical acknowledgment of the arbitrary nature of the choice reflects his persistent attention to opportunities for individuals to see identity formation as a creative undertaking.

De Quincey had a limited acquaintance with his father, whose business kept him away from home for extended periods prior to his death from consumption in 1793. This death was the third that De Quincey experienced in early childhood; his older sister Jane had died in 1790, and his sister Elizabeth, with whom he was particularly close, died in 1791. This series of events established an understanding of life as uncertain and transitory at an early stage in De Quincey's life. The loss of Elizabeth's companionship also contributed to the development of his later tendency to withdraw from social activity into the realm of his own subjectivity, which included an intense interest in the significance of dreams: "Now began to unfold themselves the consolations of solitude, those consolations which only I was destined to taste; now, therefore, began to open upon me those fascinations of solitude, which, when acting as a co-agency with unresisted grief, end in the paradoxical result of making out of grief itself a luxury; such a luxury as finally becomes a snare, overhanging life itself, and the energies of life, with growing menaces" ("Affliction" 45). This passage points toward De Quincey's emphasis on a visionary subjectivity, what Robert Morrison describes as a "constitutional determination to reverie" (*English Opium-Eater* 110), which becomes such a major theme in De Quincey's life and work. De Quincey's writings about those encounters and their effect on him also exemplify the leisurely exploration of the individual imagination that De Quincey identified as a central feature of rhetoric, the Romantic solitude that Camlot contrasts with "the practical solitude and isolation" that De Quincey experienced as part of his existence as a periodical writer (86).

In addition to the psychological effects of these early-childhood losses, the death of De Quincey's father had important material consequences for Thomas's life. Although the elder Quincey's travel schedule had prevented him from forming close personal relationships with his children, he did provide for them and maintained careful oversight of decisions concerning their upbringing. Under the terms of his will, five guardians were appointed to guide the children to adulthood, a group comprising his wife and four of his close friends. De Quincey's relationship with his guardians, including his mother, was complicated and not always tranquil. Mrs. Quincey's strong personality, austere evangelical views, and determination to control her children led to frequent skirmishes with a son who had a definite sense of his own talents and preferences. The death of De Quincey's father therefore required him to engage in an ongoing struggle to assert himself in the face of his mother's powerful will and cope with the consequences of poor financial management on the part of his guardians. Mr. Quincey's business acumen was evident in the stability of his business at the time of his death and in the careful provisions he made for his family. Unfortunately, the guardians were less shrewd in their management of Mr. Quincey's financial affairs.

In addition to the dwindling De Quincey fortune, Thomas had to contend with frequent conflicts with his guardians over his education. His guardians took a strong interest in making sure that De Quincey received a good education, but they were not always as imaginative in working with him as they might have been. A creative approach would have been valuable in De Quincey's particular case, given that his extraordinary intellect and sensitive disposition did not make him immediately amenable to traditional educational choices. Moreover, his confidence in his own judgment in intellectual matters caused him to be unwilling to yield to those with whom he disagreed. The complicated interpersonal dynamic between De Quincey and his guardians, alongside his personal idiosyncrasies, persistently affected the education he received. The result was a rather unorthodox academic career. There were some brilliant successes, particularly in the area of classical languages, for which by all accounts De Quincey had an unusual aptitude. However, his education was also marked by periodic lapses in formal instruction and by frequent transfers from one school to another. These patterns of interruption created challenges that were exacerbated by De Quincey's general detachment from most of the institutions where he found himself, due to his determination to pursue education on his own terms, unfettered by those whom he considered his intellectual inferiors.

De Quincey's early education was directly supervised by one of his guardians, the Reverend Samuel Hall, who began to tutor De Quincey and his brother soon after Mr. Quincey's death. De Quincey studied Latin and Greek on weekdays and on Sundays listened to Reverend Hall's sermons, which he was required to summarize thoroughly and accurately as part of his lesson for the next day. The *Confessions* contains a scathing assessment of Reverend Hall's uninspired preaching and an account of De Quincey's dread of the weekly ordeal of committing Hall's sermons to memory:

> [E]very sermon in this morning course was propounded to me as a textual basis upon which I was to raise a mimic duplicate—sometimes a pure miniature abstract—sometimes a rhetorical expansion, but preserving as much as possible of the original language, and also (which puzzled me painfully) preserving the exact succession of the thoughts; which might be easy where they stood in some dependency upon each other, as, for instance, in the development of an argument, but in arbitrary or chance arrangements was often as trying to my powers as any feat of rope-dancing. (239)

Yet, De Quincey was able to conclude in later life that the discipline Hall forced upon him did help to develop his exceptional mental powers, particularly in the area of memory: "[I]t ripened into a great advantage for me, though long and bitterly I complained of it, that I was not allowed to use a pencil in taking notes: all was to be charged upon the memory. But it is notorious that the memory strengthens as you lay burdens upon it, and becomes trustworthy as you trust it" (240).

De Quincey's study with Hall ended in 1796 when Mrs. Quincey moved to Bath. After joining her there, he spent three fairly happy years studying at the Bath Grammar School, where he distinguished himself by his remarkable proficiency in Greek and Latin. However, he was injured at school in early 1799 when he was accidentally hit on the head by a cane directed at a group of students who were misbehaving during a teacher's absence from the classroom. Although the doctors who attended him seem to have taken the illness seriously, biographer Grevel Lindop suggests that the injury was probably fairly minor (25–26), an interpretation supported by De Quincey's later reflections. (In "I Am Introduced to the Warfare of a Public School," De Quincey remembers, "From the Bath Grammar School I was removed in consequence of an accident, by which at first it was supposed that my skull had been fractured; and the surgeon who attended me at one time talked of trepanning. This was an awful word: but at present I doubt whether in reality anything very serious had happened" [159].) Although he expected to return to school after his convalescence, his mother abruptly decided to remove him from the school without providing him with a direct explanation of her decision.

De Quincey's interpretation of this incident illustrates his perception that his mother's evangelical zeal compromised her interest in his academic training by allowing her concerns about discipline and pride to interfere with her appreciation of her son's accomplishments and vision of his future. De Quincey explains that his mother's decision was the result of a visit from the headmaster and his associates, who had come to the De Quincey house "requesting earnestly, in terms most flattering to myself, that I might be suffered to remain there. . . . [I]t illustrates my mother's moral austerity that she was shocked at my hearing compliments to my own merits, and was altogether disturbed at what doubtless these gentlemen expected to see received with maternal pride. She declined to let me continue at the Bath School" ("I Am Introduced" 160). Although De Quincey never abandoned his Christian upbringing, his frustration at the restraints his mother's extreme evangelical views imposed on his education undoubtedly supported De Quincey's desire to avoid the type of dogmatic excess he found in his mother's version of religion.

A few months later, De Quincey's mother decided that he should pursue his education at the Winkfield Academy, a small institution that Thomas found far inferior in quality to the Bath Grammar School, noting that its chief benefit from his mother's standpoint lay in "the religious character of the master" ("I Am Introduced" 160). It was during this period that

De Quincey discovered the writings of Wordsworth and Coleridge, who would become two of his most significant intellectual influences. Morrison suggests that De Quincey found the *Lyrical Ballads* so compelling because they offered a vision of the world that supported De Quincey in seeking possibilities beyond the confines of his mother's staunch Evangelicalism and discovering meaning after the sorrows of his early years (*English Opium-Eater* 35–36). This encounter convinced him of the profound literary merits of Coleridge and Wordsworth and launched De Quincey's plans to produce writing influenced by the work he so admired (Morrison, *English Opium-Eater* 35–36).

De Quincey's study at Winkfield ended in 1800, when his mother and guardians enrolled him in the Manchester Grammar School. The primary purpose of this change was to make Thomas eligible for a scholarship to Oxford available to students who had completed three years' residence at Manchester, but he was unimpressed by the pecuniary advantage in juxtaposition to what he perceived as the school's academic inadequacies. His description of his arrival at the school captures the physical and intellectual desolation he experienced in his new surroundings: "Puritanically bald and odious, therefore, in my eyes, was the hall up which my guardian and myself paced solemnly—though not Miltonically 'riding up to the Soldan's chair,' yet, in fact, within a more limited kingdom, advancing to the chair of a more absolute despot" (*Confessions* 248). The despot in question was the headmaster, Charles Lawson, whom De Quincey describes with typical incisiveness: "Life was over with him, for its hopes and for its trials. Or at most one trial yet awaited him; which was—to fight with a painful malady, and fighting to die. He still had his dying to do: he was in arrear as to *that:* else all was finished" (249; original emphasis).

De Quincey's subsequent experiences substantiated his negative impression of the school. To be sure, his account in the *Confessions* of the time he spent at Manchester contains positive statements about his life there, particularly with regard to fellow students: "I felt more respectfully towards the majority of my senior school-fellows than ever I had fancied it possible that I should find occasion to feel towards any boys whatever. My intercourse with those amongst them who had any conversational talents greatly stimulated my intellect" (269). He later adds, "I acknowledge, with deep self-reproach, that every possible indulgence was allowed to me which the circumstances of the establishment made possible" (270). Nevertheless, De Quincey was deeply unhappy with the school, a situation health problems aggravated and that he blamed on Lawson's regimen, which featured long hours of study without adequate exercise and fresh air, and on the inferior medical treatment he received from the "medical ruffian" who attended him (272).

By early 1802, De Quincey had made his dissatisfaction known to his mother, who refused to listen to his pleas to be allowed to leave the school. Their correspondence during this period chronicles an ongoing conflict on this subject. Although De Quincey presented what he believed to be a persuasive argument in favor of his departure from Manchester, his mother was completely unmoved by his pleas. However, he was not to be dissuaded from the view that he could no longer tolerate the school. Since his mother refused to listen to what he perceived as the solid evidence supporting his desire to leave, he decided to take matters into his own hands and depart from the school at the earliest opportunity:

> Such an instinct it was, such a rapturous command—even so potent, and alas! even so blind—that, under the whirl of tumultuous indigna-tion and of new-born hope, suddenly transfigured my whole being. In the twinkling of an eye, I came to an adamantine resolution—not as if issuing from any act or any choice of my own, but as if passively received from some dark oracular legislation external to myself. That I would elope from Manchester—this was the resolution. (*Confessions* 278)

De Quincey acted on his resolve in July 1802, when he made his escape from Manchester Grammar School during the night.

Although his mother was severely displeased, her brother persuaded her to grant De Quincey a small allowance to begin a walking tour of Wales. De Quincey's travels seem to have been generally successful. He carefully managed his money by staying at inexpensive lodgings and occasionally sleeping in the open air. This experience gave him opportunities to cultivate the conversational skills for which he later became famous; he cheerfully notes that those skills ensured his popularity in the various places where he stopped, and he refers to several friends who took an interest in his welfare. At the same time, De Quincey's somewhat nervous temperament led to misunderstandings and other difficult moments in his travels.

One such misunderstanding was with his landlady, an event that led De Quincey summarily to quit his lodgings and begin wandering through Wales without permanent housing. Although for a time he was able to find satisfactory temporary lodgings as he moved from place to place, he grew tired of the economy and simplicity of his existence and longed for a wider variety of experience. His decision to travel to London was based at least partly on his belief that doing so would be financially advantageous, a surprising assessment in light of the fact that this change in plans required him to give up his allowance. The faulty reasoning by which De Quincey arrived at this decision is an early instance of the difficulty with financial management that plagued him through much of his life. It also serves as an example of the challenge he faced in attempting to reconcile his internal convictions with the realities of the external conditions that surrounded him. Extreme privation predictably marked his stay in London; for the first time he experienced genuine hunger, inadequate shelter, and life on the streets.

University Education

In March 1803, De Quincey reconciled with his family and ended his stay in London. In late December of that same year, he went to Oxford without having fully prepared for the decisions that would face him when he arrived there. He initially had no idea of which college he would enter: "I assembled all the acquaintances I had in the University, or had to my own knowledge; and to them, in council assembled, propounded my first question: What college would they, in their superior state of information, recommend to my choice?" ("Oxford" 15). De Quincey was initially drawn toward Christ Church, first because it was the largest college and might therefore support his desire to remain inconspicuous, since he reasoned that "any single member, who might have reasons for standing aloof from the general habits of expense, of intervisiting, &C., would have the best chance of escaping a jealous notice" (24). He also noted that its chapel boasted an organ and full cathedral service, which convinced him that Christ Church was "far the most splendid, both in numbers, rank, wealth, and influence" (24–25). These attractions prompted De Quincey to visit its dean, Dr. Cyril Jackson, who showed him great courtesy but informed him that prospective students must apply to Christ Church at least one year in advance (25). After a few more days of what he describes as "thoughtless indecision," De Quincey selected Worcester College, despite the fact that it lacked an organ, because it had a low entrance fee that suited his limited funds and a "reputation *at that time* for relaxed discipline" (28–29; original emphasis). There he immersed himself in a variety of intellectual pursuits but without experiencing a great deal of satisfaction with college life.

From the beginning of his time at Oxford, De Quincey's life was essentially solitary. His explanation of this rests in part on the difficulties he had encountered in his earlier life but also reflects his own romantic interpretation of those difficulties: "My eye had been couched into a secondary power of vision, by misery, by solitude, by sympathy with life in all its modes, by experience too early won, and by the sense of danger critically escaped" ("Oxford" 55). In addition to the tendency toward solitude accompanying his sensitive temperament, De Quincey struggled with strong convictions that interfered with his ability to enter into collegial relationships with his classmates, most notably his determination to pursue a curriculum more innovative than that provided at Oxford. In addition to classical languages, De Quincey had a strong interest in vernacular literature but discovered that this interest was not encouraged at Oxford and, consequently, that Oxford undergraduates were expected to know virtually nothing about English literature (57). Although he claims to understand how such ignorance might come about, he concludes that it is an "intolerable and incomprehensible" state that negatively affected his ability to relate to his peers: "In some parts, then, having even a profound knowledge of our literature, in all parts having some, I felt it to be impossible that I should familiarly associate with those who had none at all" (58, 59). De Quincey identifies his recognition of Wordsworth's greatness, which he asserts to have far anticipated the general public's appreciation of the poet's genius, as a specific and important instance of his critical skill (59).

Thus, in spite of his academic promise and keen interest in learning, De Quincey was never able to reconcile his educational goals to the structures he found at Oxford. The combined force of De Quincey's financial constraints, eccentric personality, and strong academic opinions encouraged his detachment from Oxford life: "[F]or the first two years of my residence in Oxford, I compute that I did not utter one hundred words" ("Oxford" 61). Sackville-West states that De Quincey "treated his college as a more or less inconvenient hotel, where the tuition was a hindrance rather than a help, and he left the university without taking anything from it" (72). The beginning of De Quincey's own account of his life at Oxford certainly encourages this interpretation: "Oxford, ancient Mother! Hoary with ancestral honours, time-honoured, and, haply, it may be, time-shattered power—I owe thee nothing! Of thy vast riches I took not a shilling, though living amongst multitudes who owed to thee their daily bread" (10). He explains that his inability to tolerate the intellectual weaknesses of others led him to adopt a detached stance from those for whom he could feel only contempt: "I recoiled, indeed, from the society of most men, but not with any feelings of dislike. On the contrary, in order that I *might* like all men, I wished to associate with none" (61–62; original emphasis). This attitude extended beyond fellow students to include those to whom he was expected to entrust his learning. His account of his "first (which happened also to be the last)" conversation with his Oxford tutor reveals De Quincey's impatience with any hint of carelessness in critical judgment on the part of those with whom he came in contact. He reports that the tutor's casual inquiry into his reading material had prompted him to reply that he had been reading William Paley and then adds:

> My tutor's rejoinder I have never forgotten: "Ah! An excellent author; excellent for his matter; only you must be on your guard as to his style; he is very vicious *there.*" Such was the colloquy; we bowed, parted, and never more (I apprehend) exchanged one word. Now, trivial and trite as this comment on Paley may appear to the reader, it struck me forcibly that more falsehood, or more absolute falsehood, or more direct inversion of the truth, could not, by any artifice or ingenuity, have been crowded into one short sentence. Paley, as a philosopher, is a jest, the disgrace of the age; and, as regards the two Universities, and the enormous responsibility they undertake for the books which they sanction by their official examinations for degrees, the name of Paley is their great opprobrium. But, on the other hand, for style, Paley is a master. . . . This first interchange of thought upon a topic of literature did not tend to slacken my previous disposition to retreat into solitude; a solitude, however, which at no time was tainted with either the moroseness or the pride of a cynic. (62; original emphasis)

Thus, De Quincey's encounters with members of the Oxford community strengthened his assumption that it would be best for him to rely on his own fastidious judgments, and he continued to follow a program of study that was essentially self-directed. De Quincey technically maintained his association with the institution until 1808 but was often away from the university during that period. His formal education came to an end during the final examinations that were to have earned him a degree, when he abruptly left the university immediately before the oral examination, in spite of the fact that his brilliant performance on the written portion had prompted one of his examiners to pronounce De Quincey "the cleverest man I ever met with" (qtd. in Sackville-West 93 and Lindop 160). Lindop reports that De Quincey's name was kept on the books at Oxford until 1810, which meant that he could have returned to complete his degree through that time. But he did not choose to do so.

For all the limitations De Quincey encountered during his years at Oxford, he did not waste the years he spent there. The curriculum he designed for himself consisted of an ambitious array of texts, ranging from Greek and Latin to philosophy and literature. Sackville-West reports that "if the society of the place had no charms for him, the passion for work caught him up like a blast of wind and whirled him away. In those first two years at Oxford he worked harder than he had ever done before, thus acquiring the habits of inexhaustible memory and concentration that afterwards proved his main assets in life" (74). Morrison reports that his most frequent companion was a German named Schwartzburg, who provided instruction in Hebrew and helped him acquire greater proficiency in German. He also began a reading program modeled on Coleridge's interests, which immersed him in German philosophy (Morrison, *English Opium-Eater* 101). Although he initially had great enthusiasm for Immanuel Kant, De Quincey explains that he quickly became disenchanted with what he saw as Kant's pessimistic view of humanity, concluding that Kant's philosophy was "a philosophy of destruction, and scarcely in any one chapter so much as *tending* to a philosophy of reconstruction" ("German Studies" 86; original emphasis). In spite of this negative judgment, De Quincey continued his interest in Kant and German metaphysics throughout his lifetime, as is evident in his translations of the works of German writers for British periodicals.

De Quincey's Circle

Given De Quincey's avid interest in English literature and Romantic poetry, it is not surprising that he carefully cultivated a circle of acquaintances that included a number of prominent writers of his day. Although generally shy and retiring, he sometimes took bold steps to obtain introductions to those whose work interested him. Morrison notes that De Quincey's 1803 diary reflects his interest in "patterning his self—or more especially, his potential self—on Coleridge" (*English Opium-Eater* 83), a goal that in 1804 led De Quincey to cultivate an acquaintance with Charles Lamb in hopes that this would lead to an introduction to Coleridge (Sackville-West 80; Morrison, *English Opium-Eater* 112–13). Although the hoped-for introduction did not come about following this visit, De Quincey again pursued a meeting with Coleridge in the summer of 1807, when he traveled to the home of Coleridge's close friend Thomas Poole in hopes of finding the poet there. After staying with Poole for several days, he went on to Bridgewater, where he finally met Coleridge, whom he recognized due to the "peculiar appearance of haze or dreaminess" in the poet's eyes ("Samuel Taylor Coleridge" 150). De Quincey interrupted Coleridge's reverie to introduce himself but found that Coleridge initially seemed baffled, uttering "rapidly a number of words which had no relation to either of us" ("Samuel Taylor Coleridge" 150). However, Coleridge soon came to himself, responded graciously to De Quincey, and eventually invited him to dine in his home, which began De Quincey's long acquaintance with Coleridge and his family. De Quincey spent much time with Coleridge at his home in Bristol, where they discussed shared interests that included history, German metaphysics, and opium (Morrison, *English Opium-Eater* 122).

On other occasions, De Quincey's reticence did slow his progress in developing the literary connections he sought. In 1803, he sent a letter to Wordsworth, articulating in fervent terms his appreciation for Wordsworth's poetry and indicating a desire for a meeting, and Wordsworth responded with an open invitation for De Quincey to visit his home. Although De Quincey made two trips from Oxford to the Lake District in 1806 to follow up on this offer, he found himself too filled with awe to approach Wordsworth: "The very image of Wordsworth, as I prefigured it to my own planet-struck eye, crushed my faculties as before Elijah or St. Paul" ("Lake Poets: William Wordsworth" 231). His acquaintance with the Coleridge family finally provided De Quincey with the opportunity to meet Wordsworth. During a visit in 1807, De Quincey learned that a lecture engagement would prevent Coleridge from accompanying his family on an upcoming trip through the Lake District ("Lake Poets: William Wordsworth" 233). De Quincey offered to escort the family, which provided a natural means of introduction to the Wordsworths, an event that, even so, was "marked by a change even in the physical condition of my nervous system" ("Lake Poets: William Wordsworth and Robert Southey" 303).

De Quincey spent several days with the Wordsworths and accompanied the group on a visit to the home of Robert Southey, whom De Quincey describes as "the most industrious of all literary men on record" ("Lake Poets: Wordsworth and Southey" 318). His stay with Southey not only made him aware of opportunities to make a living through journalism but also broadened his horizons politically (319). Although De Quincey notes that he had little familiarity with politics at that time, his general outlook included "a frenzied horror of jacobinism" (322). His observation of a political conversation between Wordsworth and Southey challenged his assumptions: "[I]t sounded as a novelty to me, and one which I had not dreamed of as a possibility, to hear men of education and liberal pursuits—men, besides, whom I regarded as so elevated in mind, and one of them as a person charmed and consecrated from error—giving utterance to sentiments which seemed absolutely disloyal" (322). In spite of what he describes as the sorrow he felt upon hearing criticisms of the royal family on that occasion, De Quincey found his encounters with these literary men tremendously stimulating and continued his friendship with both for years afterward.

His obligations at Oxford gave him only a week to spend with the Words-worths during his first visit in 1807 ("Saracen's Head" 348). In November 1808, he returned for a longer visit at the family's new home, Allan Dale, and the following February, De Quincey took a seven-year lease on Words-worth's cottage at Grasmere ("Saracen's Head" 358–59). Although Lindop describes Wordsworth as "just a shade reserved" toward De Quincey (162), he was warmly welcomed by Wordsworth's sister Dorothy and developed a close relationship with the Wordsworth children. De Quincey reports that he saw Coleridge almost every day during that period and lent him numerous volumes from his extensive library of German books ("Samuel Taylor Coleridge" 191). During that period, he also met a lifelong friend, the writer John Wilson, who had been his contemporary at Oxford but whom he had not met there.

De Quincey's association with Wordsworth gave him an opportunity to revise, edit, and oversee the publication of Wordsworth's *Convention of Cintra* pamphlet, an argument against the British decision to sign an agreement that allowed Napoleon's defeated troops to withdraw from Portugal with their belongings and plunder from the war. Sackville-West expresses surprise at the fact that Wordsworth would entrust such a task to the young De Quincey but concludes that Wordsworth must have shared Coleridge's appreciation for De Quincey's "critical faculties," an assessment later supported by Wordsworth's request for De Quincey's judgment of *Laodamia* (111). De Quincey faced numerous challenges in negotiating his role as editor. Margaret Russett observes that "from the beginning, he was caught between the equally untenable alternatives of delaying progress by deferring to Wordsworth, or second-guessing the author's 'will' by assuming local authority. Given a choice between two evils, De Quincey incurred the consequences of both" (83). Russett explains that De Quincey's work slowed progress on the pamphlet and also altered some of the fundamental premises of Wordsworth's argument: "De Quincey's zealous attention to detail looked to Wordsworth like so much rotten custom and precedent, a busy and purblind display of impedimenta. His every attempt to rephrase the manuscript or to assert editorial prerogative was regarded by the poet as an irruption of noisy subjectivity into the impersonal current of true feeling" (87). It may have been this quality that Coleridge criticized in describing the stylistic flaws that came about from De Quincey's "strange and most mistaken System of punctuation" (qtd. in Sackville-West 112; Morrison, *English Opium-Eater* 145). Morrison argues that the problems with the pamphlet's production can be attributed to both Wordsworth and De Quincey; while he acknowledges that "De Quincey was not well suited to smooth progress in business," he adds, "Wordsworth had made a difficult job much worse with his arrogance and insensitivity" (*English Opium-Eater* 145–46). Regardless of where the blame for the pamphlet's production delays may lie, the pamphlet was not a bestseller, and De Quincey never collaborated with Wordsworth again (Russett 87–88).

Notwithstanding this unsatisfactory attempt at a literary partnership, De Quincey continued his close association with the Wordsworth family for some years. However, gradual erosion took place. Lindop emphasizes two circumstances that negatively affected the relationship: the escalation of De Quincey's use of opium in 1814 (203) and his romance with Margaret Simpson, the daughter of a neighboring farmer, which began in 1815 (215). De Quincey engages directly with this development in his essay titled "Gradual Estrangement from Wordsworth," originally part of an article titled "Walking Stewart" published in an 1840 issue of *Tait's Magazine*. At the beginning of that article, De Quincey acknowledges that he never fully penetrated Wordsworth's reserve: "Men of extraordinary genius and force of mind are far better as objects for distant admiration than as daily companions" (197). De Quincey describes himself as having patiently accommodated his friend's personality quirks: "Upon ground where he was really strong, Wordsworth was not arrogant. . . . [T]here *were* fields of thought or of observation which he seemed to think locked up and sacred to himself" (198; original emphasis). De Quincey insists that he took upon himself much of the burden of maintaining cordial relations by avoiding topics that would encourage Wordsworth's demonstration of "ungenial and exclusive pride" (199), a quality evident in instances where Wordsworth made negative pronouncements about "many books which I had been accustomed to admire profoundly" (204).

In addition to being unable to confide fully in Wordsworth about books and ideas, De Quincey laments the lack of open communication about the kinds of disagreements that arise between people who associate with each other on a daily basis. While some of De Quincey's criticisms capture character traits in Wordsworth that are documented elsewhere, it would have been hard for anyone to live up to the idealized image De Quincey had developed of Wordsworth before they had even met for the first time.

Morrison comments, "Thomas had very high expectations of the poet right from the start, and they never ceased to burden his relationship with him" (*English Opium-Eater* 91). De Quincey maintains that Wordsworth's unwillingness to discuss matters of personal injustice or to listen to explanations that would clear up misunderstandings presented an obstacle to their continued association. At this point, he acknowledges that his attempt to forge a strong friendship with Wordsworth had never been truly successful due to Wordsworth's tendency to remain aloof: "[I]n reality, never after the first year or so from my first introduction had I felt much possibility of drawing the bonds of friendship tight with a man of Wordsworth's nature. He seemed to me too much like his own Pedlar in the 'Excursion,' a man so diffused amongst innumerable objects of equal attraction that he had no cells left in his heart for strong individual attachments" ("Gradual Estrangement" 202). De Quincey insists that these frictions did not entirely alter his positive assessment of Wordsworth's artistry; however, they did throw him into a state of confusion: "For some years, so equally ineradicable was either influence—my recollection, on the one hand, of the books despised, and of their power over my feelings; on the other, my blind and unquestioning veneration for Wordsworth—that I was placed in a strange sort of contradictory life; feeling that things were and were not at the same instant; believing and not believing in the same breath" ("Gradual Estrangement" 204).

De Quincey acknowledges that their personal differences ultimately tarnished his admiration for Wordsworth, leaving him disillusioned that the person whom he had held in such high esteem had proven to have flaws:

> [I]t may well be understood that, by these striking instances of defective sympathy in Wordsworth with the universal feelings of his age, my intellectual, as well as my personal, regard for him, would be likely to suffer. In fact, I learned gradually that he was not only liable to human error, but that, in some points, and those of large extent, he was frailer and more infirm than most of his fellow-men. I viewed this defect, it is very true, as being the condition and the price, as it were, or ransom, of his own extraordinary power and originality; but still it raised a curtain which had hitherto sustained my idolatry. I viewed him now as a *mixed* creature, made up of special infirmity and special strength. And, finally, I now viewed him as no longer capable of an equal friendship. ("Gradual Estrangement" 206; original emphasis)

Thus, De Quincey confirms in writing a decline in his relationship with the Wordsworths that had taken place over several years.

Even as De Quincey's relationship with the Wordsworths cooled, his experience with the wider literary world continued to develop. In 1814, he visited Wilson in Edinburgh and became part of a circle of future prominent writers. Lindop states, "Edinburgh gave him the company and stimulation he had begun to lack at Grasmere" (213), and for the most part, De Quincey appears to have been respected for his intellect and stimulating conversation. At the same time, J. G. Lockhart's reference in a letter to De Quincey as "a most strange creature" (qtd. in Lindop 214) suggests that De Quincey's eccentricities continued to be evident, even in circles generally appreciative of his brilliance.

In addition to these changes in his literary connections, De Quincey's personal life altered in significant ways during the second decade of the nineteenth century. Margaret Simpson gave birth to their son William on November 15, 1816, and she and De Quincey married in February of the following year. Morrison notes that De Quincey recognized and even appreciated the disparity between Margaret's education and his own but adds, "Morally and emotionally, however, De Quincey exalted Margaret, for he saw her as in possession of the innate nobility that he frequently associated with the lower classes" (*English Opium-Eater* 167). Yet, although De Quincey might have seen himself to be "following good Wordsworthian lore" in rejecting class distinctions for the sake of love, his relationship with Margaret apparently contributed to a further decline in his relationship with the Wordsworths (Morrison, *English Opium-Eater* 166, 181). However, De Quincey's assessment of Margaret's nobility seems to have been accurate, as she provided him with a constant and stabilizing presence through the severe challenges that lay ahead.

De Quincey the Opium-Eater

The events of De Quincey's life can be seen as both shaping and reflecting his developing character, and his character in turn has a significant influence on his critical perspective. The seeds for his interest in a notion of rhetoric that involves expansive intellectual activity and a luxurious exploration of ideas can be found in his individualized educational program, a lifelong preoccupation with dreams, and the cultivated sensibility that he describes in the diary he composed at Everton immediately after his London experience: "A few days ago . . . I became fully convinced that one leading trait in my mental character is—*Facility of Impression*. My hopes and fears are alternately raised and quelled by the minutest—the most trivial circumstances—by the slightest words. . . . Above all, witness the strong effects which striking descriptions of the *new sort* have. . . . —To me these are always paintings. Thus is my understanding triumphed over by my heart" (qtd. in Lindop 106, original emphasis). At this point in De Quincey's life, he perceives education as achieving success "by producing on the mind these two effects 1. Continually calling forth (and thus invigorating) the passions; 2. By relieving—varying—and so rendering more exquisite those fits of visionary and romantic luxuriating or of tender pensive melancholy—the necessary and grand accompaniments of that state of mind to which this system of education professes to lead" (qtd. in Lindop 98). The Romantic impulse that De Quincey acquires early in life continues to manifest itself later in his theories of language and in the literary texts he produces.

An additional influence on De Quincey's personal development and writing, and the one for which he is perhaps most famous, was opium, which he took for the first time in the autumn of 1804 while visiting London from Oxford. This turning point in De Quincey's life originated in his unusual views of medicine. He explains that he attributed a bad toothache he developed that autumn to a recent lapse in his daily practice of washing his head in cold water, which he resumed one night before he went to bed. After sleeping with his head drenched in cold water, De Quincey awoke with severe rheumatic pains in his head and jaw, which continued to plague him for the next twenty days (*Confessions* 379). The severity of his situation caused him to purchase opium, which someone at Oxford had recommended as a useful pain remedy. After using opium on an occasional basis for some years, "a most appalling irritation of the stomach" led him in 1813 to become "a regular and confirmed opium-eater" (398, 400). Soon after he began this daily habit, his use of opium escalated to 320 grains (eight thousand drops) per day. He managed in a short time to reduce his intake to 40 grains (one thousand drops) per day, which he describes as giving him great happiness (402), but a few years later, his opium intake reached an even more significant crisis point. During 1817 and 1818, De Quincey's escalated opium use caused him to be debilitated by horrifying visions, often based on images from troubling incidents in his early life, which made him afraid to sleep and unable to write. His wife saw him through these long and troubling nights and supported him as he worked his way back to another period of greater tranquility. De Quincey's dependence on opium waxed and waned throughout his life from that point forward. He describes the pattern by which he periodically moved toward "reconquering the ground which I had lost" (417) once he had reached the point where excessive quantities of opium had made his life unbearable but adds, "But what followed? In six or eight months more, upon fresh movements arising of insupportable nervous irritation, I fleeted back into the same opium lull. To and fro, up and down, did I tilt upon those mountainous seas, for year after year" (417).

In spite of his struggles with dependency, De Quincey was able to return to work after each crisis, a necessity in light of his growing family and shrinking resources. In July 1818, he assumed editorship of the *Westmorland Gazette*, a post he held just over a year. Sackville-West attributes De Quincey's lack of success in this position to his inability to understand his audience: "Not only were his own contributions to the paper absurdly learned and above the heads of the general public, but the matter which he included from other sources was altogether too idiosyncratic to meet the taste and requirements of his subscribers" (163). Lindop offers another interpretation, based on the poor fit between De Quincey's temperament and the duties required of a periodical editor: "There is no indication that the proprietors objected to De Quincey's filling the *Gazette* with murder trials and essays on Kant. . . . He lost his job through a combination of practical inefficiency and over-sensitivity to the attacks of the rival newspaper" (236).

The short duration of De Quincey's editorial career further aggravated the financial woes that had plagued him through most of his life. While De Quincey's financial instability had in some respects begun with the depleted resources caused by the poor management of his guardians, it was unquestionably made worse through what his daughter Florence describes as "an absolutely childish incapacity for business" ("[Correspondence between Mrs. Bairdsmith and John Blackwood]"), as well as his periods of heavy opium use. In an 1890 letter to the editor of *Macmillan's*, Florence defends De Quincey's ability to support his family through his writing, although she goes on to acknowledge, "No doubt there were times (most annoying to publishers I am sure) earlier when the tyranny of opium overcame him and grievous sorrows seemed to numb his powers; but the time was wondrously short, when one considers the delicate nervous organization that had to be struggled with before he was again at work upon his almost ceaseless labor."

This passage aptly describes the alternation of periods of indolence with frenzied journalistic activity that De Quincey's excessive opium use brought on. Although Morrison notes that "De Quincey was thoroughly undisposed to sell his knowledge for money" (*English Opium-Eater* 184), the need to support his family ultimately overcame such scruples. De Quincey's complete commitment to a career as a journalist followed his failure as an editor, and his path to success as a writer was filled with challenges that help to explain the ambivalence toward the periodical press that pervades his writing. Wilson, who had become an editor for *Blackwood's Edinburgh Magazine*, began urging De Quincey to write for *Blackwood's* in 1819, but Lindop reports that De Quincey had difficulty producing anything at that point, largely due to opium use (238–40). In late 1820, he did travel to Edinburgh and began writing for *Blackwood's*, but his relations with William Blackwood were soon strained by his erratic literary production. Blackwood's correspondence with De Quincey reveals a shifting pattern of admonition and encouragement. In an August 26, 1820, letter, Blackwood writes, "It is a remark warranted by reason, not to mention a higher sanction, that 'hope deferred maketh the heart sick.' I shall still, however, hope against hope that you will yet fulfil your long bygone engagement to the Magazine" (qtd. in Oliphant 424). A few months later, Blackwood's receipt of two pages from De Quincey causes him to write with greater optimism: "I am so happy to receive anything from you that your two pages appear like the 24 of any one else. . . . It was the knowing what you *could do* if you were once *resolved to do* which made my repeated disappointments so mortifying to me" (qtd. in Oliphant 424–25). However, by January 6, 1821, Blackwood had adopted a sterner tone: "I must tell you frankly at once that your mode of furnishing articles will neither answer your purpose nor mine" (qtd. in Oliphant 425). In De Quincey's response, written on the same day, he attempts to take control of the dialogue. Beginning on a somewhat penitent note with the acknowledgment, "I am gagged, having paid away your ten guineas, which I am now heartily sorry that ever I did," he goes on, "'A good article,' you say, 'is always in time.' Well, mine is a good one—a very good one—and therefore in time" (qtd. in Oliphant 426). A subsequent letter, written on that same day, attempts further banter, but Blackwood's response of January 8 indicates severe displeasure: "I can only excuse your letter, which I received to-day, by supposing that you were hardly awake when you wrote it" (qtd. in Oliphant 427).

In spite of the strained relationship, De Quincey maintained an intermittent connection with the magazine until Blackwood's death in 1834. Margaret Oliphant, who wrote the official history of *Blackwood's Magazine* in 1897, characterizes De Quincey's relationship with the magazine as a perpetual cycle of debt, excuses, and frantic writing: "Alas for poor De Quincey! His systematic promises, his certainties that after this one crisis is safely tided over nothing else of the kind can ever recur, his tremendous agitations and still more tremendous letter-writing, page after page in his small close handwriting, elaborate in style, always conveying another and another episode of the self-same story—never ended till his life did"

(437–38). The circumstances surrounding De Quincey's literary production, including his tense relationship with the periodical press that provided him with his livelihood, provide important insight into his insistence upon the intellectual space needed for the imaginative exploration of ideas.

Though the bitter exchanges of 1820–21 between De Quincey and Blackwood did not completely sever their connection, they did have significant consequences for both parties. De Quincey had initially planned to write *Confessions of an Opium-Eater* for *Blackwood's* but instead left Edinburgh and pursued a contract with the *London Magazine*. De Quincey's *Confessions*, his first publication for that periodical, recounts his varied experiences with opium, with a particular emphasis on the dreams the drug inspired. Published in two installments in September and October 1821 and reprinted in book form in 1822, De Quincey's *Confessions* was an immediate sensation and brought him lasting fame. His ongoing financial difficulties caused him to continue writing at a frantic pace, publishing twenty-two articles in *London Magazine* between 1822 and 1824. After Taylor and Hessey sold the *London Magazine* in 1825, De Quincey was again forced to forge a new alliance; he returned to writing for *Blackwood's* in 1826 and moved his family to Edinburgh in 1828, the year "Rhetoric" was published in *Blackwood's*.

De Quincey maintained an impressive and prolific production as a writer through much of the remainder of his life. A regular contributor to both *Blackwood's* and *Tait's Edinburgh Magazine*, he published books and essays on varied topics. Yet throughout this period, De Quincey's successes were offset by his resistance to the constraints of journalism and his awareness of the burden of writing to earn a livelihood. In 1825, he eloquently expressed this view in a letter to Wilson: "To fence with these ailments with the one hand, and with the other to maintain the war with the wretched business of hack-author, with all its horrible degradations, is more than I am able to bear" (qtd. in Lindop 277). The "horrible degradations" surrounding De Quincey's work as a journalist were therefore woven into a complicated life that included devotion to family, love of learning and literature, desire for self-expression, and addiction to opium.

De Quincey's consciousness of these "horrible degradations" and his personal aversion to the financial matters that led to his frenetic activity as a writer are reflected in his insistence upon rhetoric's detachment from the practical concerns that he perceives as a dominant force in nineteenth-century British society. It seems clear that De Quincey had no part in the "love for the practical and the tangible" that he identifies as the preoccupation of most of British society ("Style" 141); his determination to create for himself a life directed toward a power transcending such concerns infuses his theoretical approach to a rhetoric that allows for the free intellectual exploration of the creative individual. De Quincey's career as a writer for the press that he in many respects despised embodies the "paradoxical actuality of life" (Kroeber 18) that his writing explores, and the fact that De Quincey's literary production was itself driven by financial need provided him with an immediate experience of the debilitating effect of practical concerns on the free play of ideas that he considered to be the rhetorical ideal.

De Quincey's persistent financial woes were well known among his contemporaries and were a driving force in his literary production. Robert Carruthers's letter to Alexander Hay Japp reveals the immediate connection between De Quincey's writing and financial exigency:

> I had been dining one summer afternoon with William Tait, and after dinner we proceeded to Taits shop. As we went along, I observed the little man shuffling up behind us, in a loose unshaved state, wearing his list shoes. "Come on," said Tait, that is De Q. he will be wanting to borrow money. He got up to the shop door as soon as we did, entered, and succeeded in getting £2 from Tait, for which he promised to write an article for the Magazine on the Corn Laws. ("To [Alexander Hay] Japp, Inverness")

This episode illustrates De Quincey's continual struggles with debt in spite of his productivity as a writer, as well as the constant pressure to write about the immediate political affairs that were of concern to his fellow citizens. According to Lindop, he was in and out of debtors' prison nine times between 1832 and 1840 (303). After an 1837 arrest, publisher Adam Black rescued De Quincey from jail, an event Carruthers describes in the letter to Japp quoted earlier: "Adam Black told me he found the little man one day in the hands of the Sheriff's officers conveying him to Calton jail. He stopped the melancholy procession and finding the debt for which he was seized was under £30 he became responsible for it on condition of De Quincey furnishing the article on Shakespeare and Pope for the Encyclopedia [the seventh edition of the *Britannica*], which he faithfully performed." The ongoing structure of De Quincey's life consisted of writing to pay off one debt only to face the consequences of others, while his family continued to suffer from severe want in spite of his hard work—repeating the pattern that De Quincey had experienced intermittently from the time he left Manchester Grammar School. And further grief was soon to come to De Quincey, as his wife Margaret died of typhus in 1837.

De Quincey's struggles with debt and severe addiction began to diminish at the end of his life. In 1843, De Quincey moved to Lasswade, and his children's careful management gradually paid off his debts. Modest personal comfort and steady literary production characterized the final years of his life. He died in Edinburgh on December 8, 1859.

Of the facts about his life, De Quincey's difficulties with money were among those best known to his contemporaries. A survey of his daughters' correspondence reveals their justifiable satisfaction in rescuing De Quincey from his lifelong struggle with financial distress, and their determined effort to ensure that the public's memory of De Quincey focused on the stability of his final years rather than on the eccentricity and constant financial embarrassment of earlier periods. His daughter Florence was particularly energetic in challenging gossip that failed to acknowledge the change that had taken place in De Quincey's business affairs before his death, as is evident in a letter to John Blackwood in response to an unsigned article, "The Opium-Eater," by Margaret Oliphant published in the December 1877 issue of *Blackwood's Magazine*. While she demurs from questioning the article's judgments of De Quincey's literary merits, Florence adds that "the tone of this article when treating of his money affairs is such as to lead my Sister, and myself to ask you whether at his death Mr. de Quincey was in your debt, or in that of the gentleman writing the article. Mr. de Quincey himself was under the belief that he had paid off all his just debts (and we knew many unjust ones also)" ("[Correspondence between Mrs. Bairdsmith and John Blackwood]").

Although his opium use certainly accounts for much of De Quincey's difficulty handling practical matters, the more fundamental issue appears to have been one of disposition. Sackville-West notes a generous financial contribution that De Quincey when he could ill afford it presented anonymously to Coleridge, adding, "His charity, in this respect, was at all times extravagant and out of all proportion to his own assets at the moment. He disliked money intensely, with the kind of dislike generally reserved for human beings; he despised it, and apart from the necessity of buying books and, later, of keeping his family, might almost have existed without it, so absolutely unpretentious was his mode of life" (98). Even his fiercely loyal daughter admits, in a March 1886 letter to David Masson, "With all that I have said, I would not have you suppose that I am attempting to persuade you that he was not unpractical to the verge of lunacy (with the not uncommon, but most embarrassing conviction that his special strength lay in the practical) that he was not wildly imprudent, and that he was not eccentric to a degree people can-not take in, even when we set it forth in sober earnest as explaining some of his otherwise inexplicable whims and vagaries" ("[Correspondence between Mrs. Bairdsmith, Messrs]").

In spite of De Quincey's inexplicable whims and vagaries, his awareness of the wider world and his genuine interest in other people prevent him from a complete withdrawal into himself. His later insistence that rhetoric occupies a middle ground between the individual's impressions and the matters that are of interest to the external world can be seen as a feature of this combination of traits, even during those periods when he found solitude desirable. The complexity of De Quincey's character is apparent in a June 23, 1890, letter from Baird Smith to the editor of *Macmillan's Magazine*, in which she seeks to counter the public impression of her father reflected in a George Saintsbury article published in a recent issue of the magazine: "Mr. de Quincey's 'impenetrability' probably depended on his 'interviewer.' I have certainly seen him present a sphinx-like front which was sufficiently quelling to vulgar impertinence but that he was impenetrable to those who met him in simple courteous friendliness, I deny, and I should be supported by all those friends and neighbours who could pretend to intimacy with him and his family" ("[Correspondence between Mrs. Bairdsmith and the editor]"). This description of De Quincey's unusual combination of reticence and genuine interest in other people offsets to some extent the many accounts of acquaintances that focus on his strangeness and difficulty with handling ordinary social expectations. It also helps to explain the importance of his view of conversation as a vital site for public discourse, as he argues that the private sphere of conversation fosters the constructive interactions, authentic linguistic style, and thoughtful intellectual exploration that he considered to be threatened by nineteenth-century society's practical orientation.

The complexity of De Quincey's character is evident in accounts that describe him as socially uncomfortable and at the same time a charming conversationalist. In spite of De Quincey's well-known eccentricities and struggles with addiction, Baird Smith insists that his relationship with his family and friends was consistently strong. In an 1886 letter to David Masson, she writes, "[E]xcepting now and again from the necessities of business he was a man so essentially sociable that he was never separated from his family, sharing so intimately all their joys and sorrows that I never remember him absent from any event whether small, or great, and I can not point to the time when he was not in constant habits of association with some good and true friend with whom intercourse was both delightful to him and profitable" ("[Correspondence between Mrs. Bairdsmith, Messrs]").

This type of complexity also exists in the opposition between De Quincey's extraordinary productivity as a writer and the disjointed approach to his work that he demonstrates even during periods when his opium intake was not at its height, as evident in an 1856 note to James Hogg concerning his efforts to proofread his *Selections Grave and Gay*: "After fighting all night till [illegible] this morning with the torments of this Sat. attack, I fell asleep, from which sleep being awakened by the Press Messenger, I said—Come at 3. But it is now 3, and I have not been able to rise. Perhaps it will be better for me to send to the press. Or, if the press at a hazard would send down at 6, I will endeavour to be ready" ("[Autograph]"). A note dated Tuesday, October 6, 1857, reveals De Quincey's ongoing problems with management, coupled with the charm with which he dispatched his difficulties: "My dear Sir, I was shocked to find from your letter of yesterday—how very seriously I had been trespassing on your convenience, and perhaps impudent interests. By means of better [illegible] arrangements never again will I offend in *that* way. And thus there paved one extra corner of Hell. Meantime, leaving the Future and coming to the Present dilemma, in order that all my notes may not perish in most of which *Titan* has an interest greater or smaller, will you allow me 2 [illegible] viz. Wed. (to-mor.) and Thurs" ("[Autograph]"). De Quincey's eccentricity and sociability, genius and ineptitude, obsession with organization and affinity for chaos all play a part in his development of a dialogic rhetorical theory that is simultaneously grounded in tradition and radically subversive. His commitment to rhetoric as a process that explores multiple possibilities is an outgrowth of a personality that exhibits characteristics that are widely varied depending upon the interpreter, and a life embroiled in the conflicting impulses of market-driven production and intellectual play, interiority and external interests.

Embodying Rhetorical Paradox

De Quincey's complicated rhetorical theory derives from an equally complex personality. His determination to consider opposing sides is woven into the very fabric of a personality defined by paradox, a feature of De Quincey's life that Morrison aptly summarizes in the epilogue to his biography:

> Most strikingly, in the key areas of his experience, De Quincey repeatedly chose what he fought hard to overcome. He kept turning to his mother for help, even as he committed himself to throwing off her authority. He desperately wanted a close relationship with Wordsworth, but despised him for his arrogance and tactlessness. He railed against the demands

of the periodical press, but published almost everything he wrote in that medium. He struggled mightily against debt, yet rented and bought and loaned and drank in a way that ensured he would not escape it. He loved his wife and children, but placed them under unrelenting stress—including deprivations such as cold and hunger. For over half a century he championed the powers of laudanum, even as he battled again and again to renounce it. These central contradictions frustrated even his admirers. (*English Opium-Eater* 396)

Yet in the midst of a life fraught with internal and external conflicts, De Quincey achieves meaning through placing those paradoxes into a larger pattern of intellectual inquiry. The search for knowledge provides a foundation that brings together the conflicting strains in De Quincey's personality and actions. In a brief passage summarizing the critical years between 1818 and 1828, Sackville-West acknowledges that De Quincey's life can be seen as "a series of flights" but adds that such a view "lays too much emphasis on the negative aspect of De Quincey's experience, and fails to take account of the strong, if generally latent, directive strain in his character. . . . This figure . . . is simply the passion for knowledge—as learning, not as mere information" (202). Several strains of what appears to be a rhetorical theory filled with conflicting aims can be better understood when placed within a framework that brings together De Quincey's determination to escape from convention, his ongoing quest for knowledge, his desire to explore multiple possibilities, and his interest in sharing his insights with others.

De Quincey's commitment to a rhetoric that reveals the workings of an individual's internal consciousness stimulated by engagement with the external world creates a particularly significant dynamic among his life, art, and theory. His resistance to the rapid escalation of technology in his age is dynamically enacted through his work; E. Michael Thron argues that "as his public world became more graphic, useful, scheduled, and predictable, his inner world became more metaphoric, useless, and spiritually powerful" (12). De Quincey's opium use plays a role in that internal life, providing a well-known instance of artistic effort informed by personal experience. However, other areas of his life also reveal the outlines of principles developed in his rhetorical theory. His remarkable powers of conversation provided him with the basic framework for a conception of public discourse developed within a private and more sheltered environment that allows for a dialogic exchange of views that is immediate and meaningful. His unique combination of an introverted disposition with a passionate desire to acquire knowledge of the world around him contributed to his view of rhetoric as an intellectual endeavor grounded in subjectivity but accountable to a broader public. His view that society's obsession with practicality damages the intellectual vitality necessary to rhetoric can be seen as a projection of his personal frustration at the material concerns that intruded upon his intellectual work. De Quincey's life exemplifies his notion of how rhetoric works, as his private experiences are woven together to form the conceits that provide the basis for his art.

If it is rhetoric's nature to respond to the cultural conditions that surround it, the fact that De Quincey's theory is embedded in the circumstances of his life makes that theory uniquely relevant to understanding the course of rhetoric's development in the nineteenth century. A number of scholars have recognized ways in which the tensions surrounding De Quincey's life reflect the complex intersections that characterize nineteenth-century British society. In her examination of De Quincey's "minor" status in a Romantic canon that he helped to form through his role in establishing the authorial credibility of Wordsworth and Coleridge, Russett writes, "De Quincey's imbrication in the cult of self-sustaining poetic genius, on one hand, and the context of periodical writing and proto-professional criticism . . . situates him at a historical crux whose symptom, minority, is inextricable from our received narratives of greatness" (2). Thron identifies oppositions among De Quincey's Romantic vision, his representation of himself, and the financial need that drove his writing: "Although his early ambitions, rather than practice, were well within the course of a Romantic literary career . . . his pose in his first major work, the *Confessions*, is one of the author in spite of himself. . . . Throughout his career he never gave up this pose of the gentleman-scholar who writes to inform, instruct, and uplift his readers. . . . Whether this is a sensational pose, conscious or un-conscious, or an accurate reflection of what he was is complicated by his continuous need for money" (6). In a similar vein, John C. Whale describes De Quincey's work as a journalist in terms of a series of competing objec-tives: "The Romantic extremist and the essayist frequently join together to produce a crossing over of viewpoints which can be intimidating and even morally disturbing to the reader: confession and formal reticence, decadence and sentimentality intertwine in provocative ways" (35). Robert Lance Snyder acknowledges the uneven quality of De Quincey's writing but identifies integrity in "De Quincey's responsiveness to the tensions of his life and age. . . . Although besieged by debilitating self-doubt and inclined to striking defensive poses, he yet struggled with his personal anxieties, fears, and frustrations in ways that often help illuminate larger complexities of the early nineteenth century in England" (editor's introduction, xx–xxi). Snyder depicts De Quincey as embodying the turning point between Romanticism and the Victorian era: "He is, simply stated, an anomaly. But he is also one whose literary corpus comprises an elaborate, strangely protean mosaic that constantly tests our static conceptions of the man, the period, and generic boundaries—and therein lies his unique importance" (editor's introduction, xxiii). While Snyder's focus in this passage is primarily on De Quincey's literary contributions, this assessment is relevant to the study of De Quincey's rhetorical theory as well. De Quincey's awareness of the tensions inherent in the social changes that surrounded him contributes to his unique capacity for devising a rhetorical theory that responds to those changes in very particular ways. The components of De Quincey's rhetorical "mosaic" offer insight into rhetoric's flexibility in responding to social change as well as illuminating particular features that define rhetoric's transformation in the nineteenth century.

CHAPTER 3

Eddying Thoughts and Dialogical Potential

De Quincey's facility with classical languages, immersion in contemporary concerns, and unorthodox outlook are all factors in his development of a rhetoric that is grounded in earlier traditions but anticipates the changing intellectual climate of the nineteenth century. De Quincey's position as a theorist of rhetoric supports Edward Sackville-West's claim that "any attempt to fit De Quincey the writer into his period must be doomed to failure" (331). Sackville-West develops this observation by describing De Quincey as consistently moving between centuries in his intellectual interests:

> De Quincey might believe, and state, that he had never subscribed to
> Wordsworth's theory of poetic diction; but that he was obliquely affected
> by it, as by a widely diffused scent, is plain. . . . Yet the rather worried
> interest which he at all times shows in Pope, who was one of his continual
> points of reference, is evidence that the eighteenth-century "pull" was
> still strong in him, dragging him back to his earliest literary discoveries
> . . . before the nineteenth century, in the person of Wordsworth, had
> exerted its full sway over his mind and opinions. (256)

The "pull" of the eighteenth century and earlier eras is evident in De Quincey's writing about rhetoric, as well as literature, even as he advances ideas that alter rhetoric in radical ways. As the previous chapters argue, his affiliation with the periodical press also shapes his writing, as he both resists the constraints imposed upon him as a result of the venue of his publication and embraces the rhetorical possibilities available to him as a writer for periodicals.

One of the striking features of De Quincey's essay on rhetoric is its location in a popular magazine. While traditional rhetorical treatises had assumed their significance to a broader public, their immediate function as educational treatises created patterns of circulation that tended to be limited to narrow audiences. In contrast, De Quincey's writing participates in the formation of a new public made possible through the rise of the periodical press in the late eighteenth century. Jon P. Klancher describes this public as one that initially appeared to have limitless potential: "By representing the public sphere as a space without social differences, the periodical projects its audience as that collective formation which has momentarily displaced its own social origins—a figure which either does not actually exist or does not exist in society as presently ordered. This means the periodical text can be a space for imagining social formations still inchoate, and a means to give them shape" (24). While De Quincey's generally conservative orientation prevented him from completely embracing the democratic potential of the periodical, he was able to use the space available in periodicals to "give shape" to his own notions concerning the values that he conceived to be of fundamental importance in society's ongoing development.

As the preceding chapters point out, De Quincey's lofty intellectual aspirations early in life did not include journalism, but financial exigence pressed him to disseminate his critical reflections to the public through magazines. D. D. Devlin describes the opposition between De Quincey's image of himself and the reality of his thirty-year career as a journalist: "He saw himself as a hack in an endless struggle with deadlines, and the myth grew of a young romantic . . . whose genius was blasted by opium, poverty and the relentlessness of editors, and whose 'great intellectual project' was still-born" (1). Yet, Devlin concludes that writing for the press actually pushed De Quincey to realize his potential as a writer, noting that "it was not health or hardship which thwarted his high ambitions, but temperament. The magazines did not mar the writer: they made him" (2). In many respects, the pressure to write for an income enabled De Quincey to put his thoughts into words, and his awareness of a public forced him to demonstrate the relevance of his internal reveries to other people. Like the satirical genres described by Mikhail M. Bakhtin, the periodical publishing format "permits the author, in all his various masks and faces, to move freely onto the field of his represented world, a field that in the epic had been absolutely inaccessible and closed" ("Epic and Novel" 27). De Quincey's ability to imagine, articulate, and enact a dialogic rhetoric is ironically made possible through the publishing venue that he considered to be a constraint imposed upon the free exercise of the creative imagination.

De Quincey's Essays on Rhetoric

Due to his commitment to the effusive exploration of ideas, De Quincey's perspective on rhetoric and language can be found across a number of the essays in his extensive literary corpus. However, a number of major strains in his thinking about rhetoric are found in the five essays collected for a 1967 volume titled *Selected Essays on Rhetoric by Thomas De Quincey*, edited by Frederick Burwick. These essays, supplemented by others from De Quincey's collected works, provide the basis for the discussion of major principles of De Quincey's rhetoric found in this and the following chapter. The five essays are summarized below.

"Rhetoric"

De Quincey's essay titled "Rhetoric" was originally published in *Blackwood's Magazine* in 1828. Although this essay ostensibly offers a review of Richard Whately's *Elements of Rhetoric*, published in the same year, its primary purpose is to advance De Quincey's own singular ideas about rhetoric. Wordsworth offered a positive assessment of De Quincey's essay, although he noted that it included "some things from my Conversation—which the Writer does not seem aware of" (qtd. in Morrison, *English Opium-Eater* 260). As the first chapter notes, De Quincey maintains that his rhetoric builds upon Aristotle in addressing matters of probability. He insists that rhetoric involves neither conviction nor passion but instead requires a "coolness" that facilitates the exploration of multiple perspectives. For De Quincey, rhetoric's power emerges through the process of investigating varied possibilities, but this power has been lost due to the practical demands of a society oriented toward the immediate resolution of business matters and the scientific quest for certainty.

It is not surprising that De Quincey considered *Blackwood's* to be an appropriate venue for his essay on rhetoric. Klancher explains that *Blackwood's* objectives centered upon conservative values and ambitious intellectual engagement. He notes that *Blackwood's* "most reflexive, audience-making act was its tireless promotion of 'intellect,' or what it called the structure and workings of the human mind, as they are exhibited in its reasoning powers, in its imagination and invention, in its taste, as well as in its mode of expressing them" (52). De Quincey's essay aptly enters into this rhetorical context, as he advances ideas about rhetoric that are innovative and resistant to current trends yet framed as coherent with a revered intellectual past that he perceives to have been corrupted through the practical concerns of industrial society. Through his affiliation with a periodical dedicated to intellectual matters and the preservation of aristocratic principles, De Quincey argues for a notion of rhetoric that ironically challenges the dominance of the periodical press on which he depends for his livelihood.

"Style"

Style plays a central role in De Quincey's vision of rhetoric as an art that allows for the leisurely exploration of complex ideas through skillful language use. He articulates this relationship in "Style," published in four installments of *Tait's Magazine* between 1840 and 1841. He argues that British style had been weakened by a tendency to assume a false separation between style and substance and by an emphasis on language that supports the practical needs of business. He charges popular journalism with exacerbating the public's lack of regard for the powerful potential of language, as the haste and carelessness that typify the language found in newspapers have found their way into the discourse of ordinary people. At the same time, De Quincey suggests that publicity may serve a salutary function in the development of effective style, provided that writers take seriously their responsibility to engage with complex ideas and to conceive of language as integral to the formation of those ideas.

"Language"

The original publication venue and date for De Quincey's essay titled "Language" are not known, but the essay is included in De Quincey's *Collected Works*. Editor David Masson provides no publication material for the original essay but cites its reprint date of 1858 in De Quincey's collected writings in his footnote on the essay ("Language" 10:247). This essay reinforces a number of themes that De Quincey explores in his essays on rhetoric and style. De Quincey again asserts the integral connection between language and public life, as he offers a historical survey of changing views of language that can be accounted for by examining the evolving value systems found in various ancient and modern cultures. This historical account suggests that language use not only emerges as a response to changing cultural values but also becomes an important resource through which a society's intellectual vitality may be enhanced.

"Conversation"

In this 1847 essay, originally published in *Tait's Magazine*, De Quincey applies key insights from his theory of rhetoric to the arena of conversation. De Quincey's belief in rhetoric's responsiveness to social change is reflected in his interest in conversation. Although most of his ideas about rhetoric apply to written composition, he acknowledges the way in which skill with language can have particular social significance through the art of conversation. He insists that people should explore conversational principles more systematically due to the importance of conversation in promoting human relationships and fostering intellectual development. A skilled conversationalist himself, De Quincey insists that the sympathetic exchange of ideas created through the right exercise of private discourse can have profound consequences for individuals and society at large.

"A Brief Appraisal of Greek Literature in Its Foremost Pretensions"

De Quincey's critical review of Greek literature and oratory was published in two installments of *Tait's Magazine* in 1838 and 1839. This essay exemplifies De Quincey's goal of rhetorical practices that allow for the exploration of varied possibilities. He explains his goal as illuminating Greek language practices that counter the unexamined veneration that is often given to ancient texts. He expresses his own preference for modern writers, offering in support of this view a lengthy discussion of the benefits and challenges Greek writers and orators encountered as they responded to the specific cultural circumstances that surrounded them. Although he acknowledges positive features associated with an engagement with genuine public concerns, he argues that the depth of Greek oratory was generally diminished by the excessive zeal of Greek audiences, who were too impatient to allow for the useful digressions necessary for thorough intellectual engagement. He identifies Roman orators such as Cicero as possessing an advantage in their ability to move beyond the immediate circumstances of concern for their audiences, an advantage that he perceives to be present in the work of modern writers, as well.

As these summaries illustrate, De Quincey's discussions of language and public life center upon rhetoric's role in the development of complex ideas that can revitalize society. Key features of De Quincey's articulation of this imaginative process are explained more fully in the rest of this chapter.

Rhetoric as Intellectual Play

De Quincey's conception of rhetoric reflects both his historical consciousness and his interest in exploring rhetoric's potential to address the demands of the modern era. He recognizes that rhetorical theories and practices have historically both shaped and reflected their surrounding cultures.

He seeks to draw upon this knowledge as he traces historical developments in language use and articulates rhetoric's potential role in nineteenth-century public life. This role involves establishing a balance between individual expression and the demands of public discourse. In De Quincey's view, rhetoric's strength has always derived from the creativity of individuals. However, this creativity must take the form of intellectual engagement that requires involvement with the external world. De Quincey's emphasis on language use that weaves between objective and subjective realities parallels the two dimensions of Samuel Taylor Coleridge's theory of poetic imagination, which I. A. Richards describes as moving between the poet's inspired investigation of Nature as objective reality and the poet's construction of Nature through his writing: "1. The mind of the poet at moments, penetrating the 'film of familiarity and selfish solicitude,' gains an insight into reality, reads Nature as a symbol of something behind or within Nature not ordinarily perceived. 2. The mind of the poet creates a Nature into which his own feelings, his aspirations and apprehensions, are projected" (145). For De Quincey, as for Coleridge, language reflects the external world, but the individual's creative language use also constructs that world. De Quincey therefore envisions rhetoric as part of a dynamic process in which readers and writers develop creative forms of expression that interact with each other, reflecting the realities of their experience but altering those realities, a process that mirrors the dialogic process Bakhtin describes in which "understanding and response are dialectically merged and mutually condition each other" ("Discourse" 282). In De Quincey's view, rhetoric's value lies not in its capacity to promote the immediate resolution of public issues but in enacting a dialogic process that transforms and adds depth to the ways in which people conceive of public concerns.

De Quincey's emphasis on rhetoric's dialogic potential offers an alternative view of the historic tendency to conceive of rhetoric as an art aimed at gaining adherence from an audience. De Quincey's insistence that his own dialogical approach to rhetoric is consistent with Aristotle's rhetoric provides another instance of the paradoxes that pervade De Quincey's work, given that Aristotle's *Rhetoric* has frequently been interpreted as a central locus for a monologic rhetoric. While a number of contemporary scholars have offered readings of Aristotle that suggest that his rhetoric has a dialogical orientation, Arthur E. Walzer persuasively argues that Aristotle's view that rhetoric's purpose involves persuading an audience to adopt a particular course of action entails an approach that is audience-centered but monological (49). In explicating this position, Walzer argues that any interpretation of rhetoric must attend to the relationship between speaker and audience that it assumes; although Aristotle's rhetoric does acknowledge that the rhetor's awareness of the audience affects the message, Walzer concludes that it "is nonetheless monologic because it views the speaker's relationship to the audience as directive and unilateral, not interactive and reciprocal" (49). Walzer contrasts Aristotle's articulation of rhetoric with Bakhtin's view of dialogism, noting that "in authentically dialogic discourse, the other voice or voices cannot fall under the hegemonic control of the rhetor's ideology" (50).

In light of rhetoric's historic connection to persuasive purpose, exemplified in Aristotle's rhetoric, it is not surprising that Bakhtin contrasts rhetoric with the truly dialogic art enacted in the novel. While Bakhtin describes the novel as an "extra-artistic rhetorical genre" ("Discourse" 268), a view that acknowledges possible connections between rhetoric and dialogic activity, he also recognizes rhetoric's participation in a historical pattern that narrows the multiple voices found in language in order to advance a particular point of view: "All rhetorical forms, monologic in their compositional structure, are oriented toward the listener and his answer. This orientation toward the listener is usually considered the basic constitutive feature of rhetorical discourse. . . . This orientation toward an answer is open, blatant and concrete" ("Discourse" 280). Thus, rhetoric often becomes one discipline in which language is shaped by "*forces that serve to unify and centralize the verbal-ideological world*" ("Discourse" 270; original emphasis), as those who judge rhetoric's merits consider "only those aspects of style determined by demands for comprehensibility and clarity—that is, precisely those aspects that are deprived of any internal dialogism, that take the listener for a person who passively understands but not for one who actively answers and reacts" ("Discourse" 280). For Bakhtin, rhetoric often loses the capacity to become a dialogic encounter in the hands of the individual speaker whose attention to audience is subordinated to a predetermined purpose, a view that Walzer aptly summarizes: "For Bakhtin, then, the crucial distinction between monologic and dialogic discourse is not that in dialogic discourse the attitudes, views, and abilities of the audience shape the discourse, since this is true of virtually all language use; the crucial difference is the author's relationship to the audience—whether other attitudes, views, and abilities are honored in themselves (dialogic) or instrumental to the rhetor's purposes (monologic)" (50). In recognizing the tension between rhetoric's focus on persuasive purpose and any effort to be dialogically responsive to multiple perspectives, Bakhtin has identified a significant challenge that emerges across centuries of rhetorical history.

De Quincey confronts this challenge first through countering standard interpretations of rhetoric's monologic character and then aligning himself with the dialogic potential he finds in theorists such as Aristotle. As chapter 1 discusses, De Quincey claims a classical foundation for his notion of rhetoric, as he appropriates Aristotle's emphasis on probability in order to engage with rhetoric's capacity to negotiate among possible truths and lead people to see things in a new light. Although he defines rhetoric as the art of "giving an impulse to one side, and by withdrawing the mind so steadily from all thoughts or images which support the other as to leave it practically under the possession of a one-sided estimate" ("Rhetoric" 91), he does not consider this process to be one that denies other possibilities. Instead, De Quincey advocates an open exploration of possibility that anticipates Bakhtin's view that "the word is a mirror image of consciousness that is forever in flux" (Schuster 9). For De Quincey, intellectual flexibility is both the hallmark and outcome of the rhetorician's craft.

Although he acknowledges that his interpretation of Aristotle might be unconventional, De Quincey insists that he obtained the basic premise for his interpretation of rhetoric from "a suggestion derived from him" ("Rhetoric" 83). He maintains that Aristotle's emphasis was placed on those causes about which the understanding cannot permanently assent. According to De Quincey, Aristotle "threw the whole stress upon finding such arguments for any given thesis as, without positively proving or disproving it, should give it a colourable support" (85–86). Contrary to general opinion, he insists that the defining quality of the enthymeme lies "not in the accident of suppressing one of its propositions" (90) but in its subject matter, which deals in matters of opinion and probability.

De Quincey maintains that this subject matter gives to rhetoric a different tenor than is found in other arts. De Quincey connects with the belletristic tradition but takes it one step further in insisting that rhetoric, which he describes for the most part as a written art, is distinct from eloquence. He notes his agreement with Coleridge in dividing rhetoric and eloquence, although he denies knowledge of the precise arguments Coleridge makes in asserting the separation between the two ("Rhetoric" 92). In explaining his own position, De Quincey states that the distinction rests primarily on rhetoric's province in leading people to new insights that are available through an intellectual process removed from the emotional power associated with eloquence: "By Eloquence we understand the overflow of powerful feelings upon occasions fitted to excite them. But Rhetoric is the art of aggrandizing and bringing out into strong relief, by means of various and striking thoughts, some aspect of truth which of itself is supported by no spontaneous feelings, and therefore rests upon artificial aids" (92). De Quincey acknowledges that this definition departs from major premises held by his immediate predecessors in the rhetorical tradition. He denies both rhetoric's role in leading the audience to conviction, as articulated by Whately, and the need for rhetoric to persuade through engaging the passions, as described by George Campbell: "We, for our parts, have a third which excludes both. Where conviction begins, the field of Rhetoric ends; that is our opinion: and, as to the passions, we contend that they are not within the province of Rhetoric, but of Eloquence" (82). Thus, for De Quincey, rhetoric includes a detachment from matters that can be proven to the understanding and from resolutions that are made possible through emotional engagement. Excessive emotion not only jeopardizes the "coolness" of rhetoric but also threatens the intellectual control that De Quincey sees as a distinct feature of rhetoric, as he maintains that the quality of spontaneity that is valuable for eloquence is "death to Rhetoric" (93). In narrowing the scope of rhetoric in this way, De Quincey emphasizes its role in engaging people in critically assessing issues whose value lies in their resistance to immediate resolution, which he considers to be the key to intellectual development. Rhetoric's unique purpose lies in the use of language to guide people toward an imaginative consideration of alternate possibilities.

In spite of De Quincey's opposition to Whately and Campbell with regard to rhetoric's detachment from eloquence and conviction, his emphasis on rhetoric's relationship to probability does not in itself appear to constitute an innovation. However, the direction he takes in developing this notion involves a radical alteration in rhetoric's role in public life. In De Quincey's view, the ability to indulge freely in an exploration of possible alternatives requires a detachment from immediate everyday concerns, a step that facilitates his engagement with rhetoric as a dialogic enterprise. De Quincey insists that rhetoric "aims at an elaborate form of beauty which shrinks from the strife of business" ("Rhetoric" 93). Although he acknowledges the value of the rhetorical instruction developed by Greeks, he argues that the Romans were superior in rhetorical practice, because the Greek assemblies exhibited "fervour and . . . the coarseness of a real interest" (94), both of which "operated fatally on the rhetorician" (93–94). This example leads him to conclude that "all great rhetoricians in selecting their subject have shunned the determinate cases of real life" (4).

The ability of individual rhetors to stimulate the audience's intellect does not imply that the relationship between rhetoric and the public should be seen as one-sided, however. In De Quincey's view, rhetoric influences the public, but the public also influences rhetoric—a fact that has damaged rhetorical production in the modern era. In keeping with insights advanced by eighteenth-century rhetorical theorists such as Campbell, Hugh Blair, and Henry Home, Lord Kames, De Quincey sees all language use as responsive to cultural change, as the decisions people make about language in a given historical moment both shape and reflect the values of their surrounding cultures. His project of studying the "varying scale of appreciation applied to the diction and national language, as a ground of national distinction and honour" ("Language" 248) on the part of Greeks, Romans, French, English, and Germans in the essay titled "Language" reveals his interest in discovering the relationships between cultural evolution and the ways in which language is used in different times and places.

De Quincey acknowledges that the leisurely use of language to explore ideas has historically been a rarity and is particularly challenging in his own age. He perceives rhetoric as having great strength in the sixteenth and seventeenth centuries, "when science was unborn as a popular interest, and the commercial activities of aftertimes were yet sleeping in their rudiments" ("Rhetoric" 100). Since then, he argues, "the rhetorician's art in its glory and power has silently faded away before the stern tendencies of the age" (97). He maintains that rhetoric must be removed from "the necessities of public business" in order to thrive; its vitality depends upon the "quiescent state of the public mind . . . at leisure from the agitations of eternal change" (97). De Quincey maintains that, in an era increasingly dominated by commercial concerns, the intellectual pleasure available through rhetoric has been overwhelmed by other interests and by the constant demand for language that accomplishes immediate, practical goals.

While De Quincey's argument against rhetoric aimed at the straightforward resolution of practical goals might appear to manifest itself in an appreciation for flowery prose, this is not the case at all. He expresses his opposition to those who attend to style alone, conceiving of rhetoric as "something separable and accidental in the *manner*" ("Rhetoric" 82; original emphasis), which leads to the use of "ostentatious ornament," with the goal "not so much to persuade as to delight" (81). At the same time, he rejects the other extreme, which "lays its foundation in something essential to the *matter*" (82; original emphasis), a view that perceives rhetoric as grounded in argumentative content independent of stylistic concerns. He argues for an essential unity between matter and manner that he perceives to be inadequately recognized in the popular definitions he outlines. The next chapter discusses more fully De Quincey's conception of the integral role of style in rhetorical production.

The danger of placing too great an emphasis on matter or manner circulates throughout De Quincey's essay as he discusses the ebbs and flows of rhetoric's vitality at different historical moments, as various cultural conditions have placed too great an emphasis on style or argumentative content. He consistently criticizes the meager language that arises from the grim practicality of industrial society, a phenomenon that is not limited to Britain. He discusses the strength of French rhetoric during the reign of Louis XIV but suggests that its decline afterward is inevitable in light of the fact that "the very same development of science and public business operated there as in England to stifle the rhetorical impulses" ("Rhetoric" 121). On the other hand, De Quincey also expresses dissatisfaction with flowery prose that fails to maintain the precision necessary for the intense intellectual engagement he demands. He states that "rhetoric will not survive the age of the ceremonious in manners and the gorgeous in costume" (121) and later adds, "Florian, Chateaubriand, and others, who have written the most florid prose that the modern taste can bear, are elegant sentimentalists, sometimes maudlin and semi-poetic, sometimes even eloquent, but never rhetorical. There is no eddying about their own thoughts; no motion of fancy self-sustained from its own activities" (121). Thus, De Quincey's prescription for rhetoric involves a controlled use of language that facilitates a deep and intense exploration of thought. The "coolness of rhetoric" (96) requires a degree of detachment from the emotional outpourings that fall in the province of eloquence, but it also can only achieve its goal through a disciplined exercise of thought that probes more deeply into the conditions that have profound importance for human life.

This unity between language and thought constitutes De Quincey's adaptation of Romantic principles to rhetoric. While De Quincey's description of the cool artificiality of rhetoric departs significantly from Wordsworth's description of "good poetry" as "the spontaneous overflow of powerful feelings," his view of rhetoric's important role in promoting thorough reflection parallels Wordsworth's emphasis on the necessity of the type of careful thought that undergirds the poet's inspiration: "For our continued influxes are modified and directed by our thoughts, which are indeed the representatives of all our past feelings; and as by contemplating the relation of these general representatives to each other, we discover what is really important to men, so by the repetition and continuance of this act feelings connected with important subjects will be nourished " (preface 62). For De Quincey, as for Wordsworth, self-expression is best supported through thorough engagement with ideas.

De Quincey also engages with Coleridge's thought in using the term *eddying* to describe this type of engagement. Richards quotes two lines from *Dejection* (1802) in which Coleridge describes the imaginative activity prompted by Nature, "To thee do all things live from pole to pole / Their life the eddying of thy living soul," and goes on to explain, "*Eddying* is one of Coleridge's greatest imaginative triumphs. An eddy is in something, and is a conspicuous example of a balance of forces" (152). Yet, Coleridge's attention to this intricate balance between mind and nature does not necessarily entail an appreciation for the kind of mental activity De Quincey advocates. Coleridge's complaint that Wordsworth's writing features "occasional prolixity, repetition, and an eddying, instead of progression of thought" (*Biographia* 258) stands in contrast to De Quincey's advocacy of the power that comes from language use that involves "eddying" about one's thoughts ("Rhetoric" 121). De Quincey appropriates Coleridge's image of the "eddying" that generates meaningful experience in order to describe his own unique vision of rhetoric that stimulates the free play of imaginative inquiry.

Moreover, for De Quincey, the language of rhetoric is not identical with the "natural language of impassioned feeling" that Coleridge, referring to Wordsworth, identifies as appropriate to poetry in *Biographia Literaria* (188). In contrast, De Quincey describes rhetoric as an artificial and demanding discipline, one that "presupposes a state of tense exertion on the part both of auditor and performer" ("Rhetoric" 97). At the same time, he insists that this tense exertion is a playful and creative undertaking, as he argues that the "artifice and machinery of rhetoric furnishes in its degree as legitimate a basis for intellectual pleasure as any other" ("Rhetoric" 101). De Quincey's notion of rhetoric is in this respect aligned with Coleridge's depiction of poetry as "opposed to works of science, by proposing for its *immediate* object pleasure, not truth" (*Biographia* 172; original emphasis). De Quincey also shares Coleridge's view that writers and readers experience the power of language as they participate in a process of discovery distinct from a determined outcome: "The reader should be carried forward, not merely or chiefly by the mechanical impulse of curiosity, or by a restless desire to arrive at the final solution; but by the pleasurable activity of mind excited by the attractions of the journey itself" (*Biographia* 173). In De Quincey's view, writers and readers can only achieve the intellectual pleasure available through the rhetorical journey by maintaining a whimsical approach to the serious business of language, for "agile movement, and a certain degree of fancifulness, are indispensable to rhetoric" ("Rhetoric" 102). It is perhaps little wonder that De Quincey finds the true practice of rhetoric so rare, given that he requires that rhetoricians maintain a delicate balance of objectives that appear in many respects to oppose each other: intensity and creative freedom; serious work and pleasure; extravagant playful language and focused development of thought; subjective exploration and external stimulation; artificiality and authenticity.

The rhetorical activity outlined in De Quincey anticipates Bakhtin's description of the interplay of forces created through a dialogic use of language:

> The way in which the word conceptualizes its object is a complex act—all objects, open to dispute and overlain as they are with qualifications, are from one side highlighted while from the other side dimmed by heteroglot social opinion, by an alien word about them. And into this complex play of light and shadow the word enters—it becomes saturated with this play, and must determine within it the boundaries of its own semantic and stylistic contours. ("Discourse in the Novel" 277)

For De Quincey, as for Bakhtin, the dialogic activity of language entails the discovery of meaning available through the play of the word with light and shadow.

De Quincey's Rhetorical Criticism

Although much of De Quincey's writing about rhetoric seems abstract, he attempts to ground his ideas in observations about actual practice. In fact, De Quincey is convinced that rhetorical examples are superior to theoretical insights alone. He explains that this premise guided his classical study at Oxford, where he sought through careful study to distinguish himself from "that indiscriminate admirer of Greek and Roman literature which those too generally are who admire it at all" ("Oxford" 2:62). He argues that a true study of Greek eloquence should be based not on theory or philosophical principles but on the direct study of Demosthenes, an approach that he believes to be rare:

> I, from my childhood, had been a reader, nay, a student, of Demosthenes; and simply for this reason, that, having meditated profoundly on the true laws and philosophy of diction, and of what is vaguely denominated style, and finding nothing of any value in modern writers upon this subject, and not much as regards the grounds and ultimate principles even in the ancient rhetoricians, I have been reduced to collect my opinions from the great artists and practitioners, rather than from the theorists; and, among those artists, in the most plastic of languages, I hold Demosthenes to have been the greatest. ("Oxford" 2:63)

A similar approach guides De Quincey's investigation of rhetoric more broadly, as he consistently looks to examples to support and develop his ideas.

De Quincey identifies John Donne as "the first very eminent rhetorician in the English literature" ("Rhetoric" 100). Challenging Samuel Johnson's classification of Donne as a metaphysical poet, De Quincey argues that Donne is a consummate rhetorician who should be appreciated for the dialogical motion that characterizes his writing:

> *Rhetorical* would have been a more accurate designation. In saying *that*, however, we must remind our readers that we revert to the original use of the word *Rhetoric*, as laying the principal stress upon the management of the thoughts, and only a secondary one upon the ornaments of style. Few writers have shown a more extraordinary compass of powers than Donne; for he combined—what no other man has ever done—the last sublimation of dialectical subtlety and address with the most impassioned majesty. (101; original emphasis)

De Quincey's reference to passion along with subtlety in Donne's writings reveals that his study of rhetorical models prompts him to modify somewhat the distinction he appears to draw elsewhere between rhetorical coolness and the passionate engagement associated with eloquence. As he discusses the work of specific writers, he acknowledges that the rhetorician's art must invoke sufficient passion to hold the audience's interest. In fact, the ideal for De Quincey involves achieving a balance between rhetoric and the judicious use of eloquence, another form of the dialogic balance De Quincey advances as the guiding principle of rhetoric.

De Quincey's emphasis on rhetoric as a dialogical enterprise that promotes the investigation of multiple possibilities leads him to argue that Francis Bacon should not be accorded the status of rhetorician. De Quincey devotes a lengthy footnote to the argument that Bacon's interest in absolute truth overwhelms his otherwise promising qualities as a rhetorician:

> He had great advantages for rhetoric, being figurative and sensuous (as great thinkers must always be), and having no feelings too profound, or of a nature to disturb the balance of a pleasurable activity; but yet, if we except a few letters, and parts of a few speeches, he never comes forward as a rhetorician. The reason is that, being always in quest of absolute truth, he contemplates all subjects, not through the rhetorical fancy, which is most excited by mere seeming resemblances . . . but through the philosophic fancy, or that which rests upon real analogies. ("Rhetoric" 109n)

In the same vein, he explains that Sir Walter Raleigh possesses a different trait that interferes with rhetorical proficiency, an excessive introspection that prevents the playful engagement with the external world that is an intrinsic feature of rhetoric. De Quincey describes "the finest passages" in Raleigh's historical writing as "touched with a sadness too pathetic, and of too personal a growth, to fulfil the conditions of a gay rhetoric as an art rejoicing in its own energies" (109). Thus, De Quincey reinforces in his negative assessment of Bacon and Raleigh key premises that he had identified in his earlier explication of rhetoric's dialogic qualities: its joyous exploration of varying positions, its deliberate artificiality, and its critical engagement with the external world, even as it maintains a grounding in the creative subjectivity of the individual.

Although De Quincey's critique of Raleigh's prose is based in his assessment that rhetoric requires external stimulation to preserve its vitality and significance, he insists that plunging too fully into public life also threatens the full exercise of the rhetorician's art. He acknowledges the rhetorical skill of George Canning (1770–1827), whose four-month service as prime minister had ended in his death the year before De Quincey's "Rhetoric" was published, but criticizes him for diluting his powers due to an excessive focus on politics:

> He should have thrown himself upon the admiring sympathies of the world as the most dazzling of rhetorical artists, rather than have challenged their angry passions in a vulgar scuffle for power. In that case, he would have been alive at this hour . . . and would not, by forcing the character of rhetorician into an incongruous alliance with that of trading politician, have run the risk of making both ridiculous. ("Rhetoric" 121)

While an awareness of the concerns that are important to others lends a spark of interest to the rhetorician's oral and written discourse, to become too fully immersed in those concerns focuses the rhetorician's attention on moving to a conclusion that will immediately gratify the public's demands, rather than using the full range of language's complexity to explore varied possibilities that will challenge the public to new ways of thinking. Even pulpit oratory, which represents the supreme example of subject matter that is external to the speaker, can never be undignified but may "become unaffecting and trite unless varied and individualized by new infusions of thought and feeling" (124–25).

Although De Quincey applauds rhetorical artifice, he distinguishes between the adoption of this strategy for the purpose of intellectual growth and the political posturing that he conceives as ethically problematic. He mounts a harsh attack against noted playwright and member of Parliament Richard Brinsley Sheridan (1751–1816), whom he describes as "an absolute *charlatan* . . . the mere impersonation of a humbug" ("Rhetoric" 112; original emphasis), focusing particularly on Sheridan's conduct of the Warren Hastings impeachment as evidence of his rhetorical sterility and lack of a dialogical sensibility. While Sheridan was widely praised by contemporaries for his stirring oratory during Hastings's trial, De Quincey argues that on that occasion, Sheridan's "attempts at the grand, the pathetic, and the sentimental had been continually in the same tone of falsetto and horrible fustian" (113). By contrast, he offers high praise to Edmund Burke, whom he identifies as the "supreme writer of his century" (119), and describes him as the ideal practitioner of communication that brings together the individual's insight with broader concerns. He explains that Burke "exalted the merest personal themes into the dignity of philosophical speculations" (120). According to De Quincey, Burke possessed the rare gift of applying his creative energy not to "separable ornament," for "the fancy which he had in common with all mankind, and very probably in no eminent degree, in him was urged into unusual activity under the necessities of his capacious understanding" (115). As the next chapter discusses, De Quincey uses Burke as an example of the ideal unity of "matter" and "manner," as he demonstrates how Burke's "capacious understanding" is both developed and demonstrated through skillful and disciplined language use.

De Quincey's definition leads him to ignore much of the work that earlier thinkers describe as rhetoric, but he does include in his examples a number of writers and speakers whose work has been recognized in rhetorical history, along with others whose value to the field of rhetoric might have been previously overlooked. Throughout his discussion, De Quincey seeks to use specific examples to illuminate his complex ideas about rhetoric.

Rhetoric, Knowledge, and Power

De Quincey's study of rhetorical models leads to points of clarification in his theory, as his recognition of the rhetorician's strategic use of eloquence helps to reveal the fundamental significance of the creative dialogic enterprise made possible through rhetorical play. De Quincey's assessment of the opposition between creative inquiry and scientific knowledge is most famously articulated in two essays that outline what he conceives to be the opposition between "literature of knowledge" and "literature of power." In the first of these, "Letters to a Young Man Whose Education Has Been Neglected," first published in *London Magazine* in 1823, De Quincey sets out to clarify the varied categories of books that are commonly encompassed under the term *literature*. In setting about this task, De Quincey establishes a distinction between "Books of Knowledge" and "Literature," which he then connects to what he describes as the antithesis of knowledge, "power": "All that is literature seeks to communicate power; all that is not literature, to communicate knowledge" (10:47). Twenty-five years later, De Quincey returns to this topic in an essay titled "The Poetry of Pope," originally published in *North British Review* in 1848. Although he maintains the opposition between "knowledge" and "power," he revises the terms of his discussion in other respects, describing both types of texts as "literature" and arguing that the function of "literature of knowledge" is "to *teach*," while that of "literature of power" is "to *move*" (11:54; original emphasis). While literature of knowledge "speaks to the *mere* discursive understanding," literature of power "speaks ultimately, it may happen, to the higher understanding or reason, but always *through* affections of pleasure and sympathy" (11:54; original emphasis). Frederick Burwick notes that literary power must activate the unconscious, which will, in turn, serve as a catalyst that moves the conscious intellect to action: "De Quincey is concerned, that is, with an intense response capable of reaching through the threshold of the subconscious" (*Thomas De Quincey* 2). While De Quincey does not deny that both types of literature have important roles in human society, he strongly suggests that literature of power holds greater value: "And hence the pre-eminence over all authors that merely *teach* of the meanest that *moves*, or that teaches, if at all, indirectly *by* moving. The very highest work that has ever existed in the Literature of Knowledge is but a *provisional* work. . . . Whereas the feeblest works in the Literature of Power, surviving at all, survive as finished and unalterable amongst men" ("Poetry of Pope" 11:57; original emphasis).

As Jason Camlot notes, De Quincey is indebted to Wordsworth for the idea of drawing distinctions between literature that seeks to inform and that which sparks the creative vitality he associates with power (79). However, De Quincey's development of these principles creates some confusion. The conflicts between De Quincey's early and later discussions of the categories of literature and the blurring of the distinctions between the two categories have provoked much scholarly conversation about how De Quincey intended to define the basic terms of *knowledge* and *power*. Camlot notes that one outcome of De Quincey's delineation of these terms is to challenge the binary between literary production and criticism so that "the critic of the literature of power in much of De Quincey's writing—most obviously in his autobiographical texts—is allowed to become indistinguishable from the producer of that kind of literature" (80). De Quincey's acknowledgment that "a vast proportion of books . . . lying in a middle zone, confound these distinctions by interblending them" ("Poetry of Pope" 11:59) supports the suggestion that De Quincey avoids drawing clear lines between genres and between those who produce and receive written texts.

This confusion is particularly evident in attempting to assign rhetoric to a category, since De Quincey describes rhetoric as engaged in promoting "intellectual pleasure." Clearly, this endeavor is not strictly aligned with the pursuit of factual knowledge, but "Letters to a Young Man" establishes De Quincey's view that pleasure should not be seen as the antithesis of knowledge. However, John E. Jordan argues that the effects produced by pleasure lead people toward the heightened insight accessible through the "literature of power":

> Surely, "intellectural [sic] pleasure" is a kind of "amusement" or "enter-
> tainment" which he would call "a diluted form of the power belonging to
> passion." The very fact that he calls Rhetoric, which does not appeal to
> the emotions directly, "an inferior order" of intellectual pleasure, would
> imply that the higher orders of pleasure are closer to power. . . . Whether
> De Quincey looked to literature for power *or* pleasure, or for power in its
> pure or mixed form, it was predominantly an effect which he expected.
> And it is in this affective expectation that De Quincey's theory of lit-
> erature has a coherent center. (*Thomas De Quincey* 42; original emphasis)

In addition to the coherence based on effect that Jordan posits, De Quincey's categorization of literature achieves a degree of unity through its connection to the ancient view that rhetoric's offices are to teach, to delight, and to move. Although De Quincey's insistence that rhetoric has no connection to the passions ensures that rhetoric is not synonymous with literature of power, its role in promoting intellectual pleasure places it within the trajectory that De Quincey appropriates from the rhetorical offices and then translates into literary functions.

While De Quincey allows that particular examples of writing might mingle the categories he has devised, the extent to which he describes an opposition between the two types of literature helps to elucidate what he sees as the tension that exists between rhetoric's promise and its appropriation to serve practical needs. Wilbur Samuel Howell asserts that "De Quincey . . . would place rhetoric within the province of the literature of power" (13), but De Quincey's rhetoric hovers between knowledge and power as it circulates through the creative consciousness of the individual. De Quincey's discussion of rhetoric's decline in modern society depicts rhetoric as stalled in the pursuit of objective knowledge, which denies its proper role in weaving through the intricacies of human thoughts and leading people to new insight. He asserts that the true practice of rhetoric, which contains components of eloquence that bring rhetorical fancy to life in the lives of the rhetor and audience, generates the pleasure through language that mediates between knowledge and power. At the same time, he also points toward the danger that commercial interests and a preoccupation with science may have transformed rhetoric into a tool for merely conducting business, one example of a lesser form of language directed toward "seeking information or gaining knowledge," which De Quincey considers to be secondary to acquiring the "*power*, or deep sympathy with truth" ("Poetry of Pope" 11:55; original emphasis) available through inspiring literature. De Quincey's insistence upon the creative energy available through intellectual play with language offers rhetoric a significant role in mediating the opposition between knowledge and power in order to maintain a dynamic relationship between them. After describing De Quincey's keen awareness of "antagonisms," Burwick concludes, "As the largest and most pervasive of these contraries, knowledge and power are at work within the individual mind and within society as a whole. The province of knowledge is practical and analytic, that of power is abstract, subtle, pervasive, and profound. The categories may be opposite, but they are not mutually exclusive: power may lurk within all that is perceived as merely knowledge" (*Thomas De Quincey* 23). De Quincey's argument for avoiding rhetoric's appropriation by the practical world of "knowledge" therefore derives not from his conviction that rhetoric lies squarely in the world of "power" but from his awareness that rhetoric circulates dialogically between the two. De Quincey's rhetoric begins with a framework of existing ideas and gradually builds toward new insights that are not aimed at sparking an immediate passionate response but are instead employed in the task of subtly suggesting new possibilities and perspectives. Burwick argues that, for De Quincey, "[t]he highest form of literature is a combination of both rhetoric and eloquence brought into play by the creative genius" (xv). De Quincey's interest in intellectual pleasure reflects his sense that rhetoric maintains a vital dialectical interaction between knowledge and power, as it resists the tendency of modern society to stifle the hidden workings of power that inevitably lie beneath the practical and conscious world of knowledge.

Conversation's Role in Rhetorical Transformation

De Quincey's essay on rhetoric builds on the belletristic tradition in a number of important respects. De Quincey's division between rhetoric and eloquence implicitly makes the written text more central to rhetoric than oratory. His reliance on criticism to illustrate his ideas about rhetoric also carries forward the approach found in Blair's *Lectures on Rhetoric and Belles Lettres*. De Quincey's view that rhetoric is grounded in the subjectivity of individuals willing to engage in "eddying about their own thoughts" also places an emphasis on writing. Most important, his description of the rhetorician's art as based in a fanciful enterprise detached from the resolution of immediate concerns connects rhetoric primarily to writing rather than public speaking.

Given De Quincey's unusual perspective on rhetoric, it is not surprising that one genre of spoken language that closely connects to his notion of rhetoric has not traditionally been classified as part of the rhetorical tradition: conversation. De Quincey's essay titled "Conversation," published in *Tait's Magazine* in October, 1847, demonstrates a number of parallels between what he conceived to be good conversational practice and the guidelines for rhetoric he had outlined almost twenty years previously. For De Quincey, conversation, like rhetoric, engages the individual in freely exploring subjective insights that provide the basis for intellectual stimulation. Conversation has a particularly significant place in De Quincey's vision of a dialogic rhetoric since successful conversation by nature illustrates language that is enhanced as the speaker's "orientation toward the listener is an orientation toward a specific conceptual horizon, toward the specific world of the listener" (Bakhtin, "Discourse" 282). For De Quincey, conversation must not illustrate Bakhtin's concern about communication styles that "take the listener for a person who passively understands but not for one who actively answers and reacts" ("Discourse" 280). He insists that conversation must not become a stale monologue in which the speaker advances positions without regard for the audience's active participation, anticipating Bakhtin's recognition that "insofar as the speaker operates with such a passive understanding, nothing new can be introduced into his discourse" ("Discourse" 281).

De Quincey's unique vision of rhetoric as an encounter with varied interpretations establishes a clearer connection between rhetoric and conversation than is assumed by rhetoricians who define rhetoric in terms related to persuasive civic action and judgment. While Thomas Farrell acknowledges "the interdependence of the conversational and the rhetorical genre" (233), he identifies each as having a distinct form and function: "[O]ne presents itself as monologic, partisan, and directed outward to the attention of others, who then judge its quality; this is the performative dimension of rhetoric. The other appears to be dialogic, bipartisan, and directed only to those in the immediate encounter, who may appreciate, but never fully grasp, the holistic form itself" (236). Although Farrell has aptly described distinctions that are present in many conceptions of rhetoric and conversation, De Quincey's view that rhetoric is not necessarily "monologic, partisan, and directed outward to the attention of others" blurs the traditional boundaries that Farrell delineates between these two forms of discourse. In De Quincey's view, conversation reflects rhetoric's capacity to promote a dialogic encounter with alternative positions, an enterprise that can positively affect public discourse even as it is grounded in private discursive practices. De Quincey's explication of conversation's social role reflects his conviction that rhetoric achieves vitality through individuals whose expressions infuse the social world with a creative subjectivity that consciously interacts with other voices and perspectives, countering the trend toward utility that he sees as a dominant feature of nineteenth-century society. Burwick describes De Quincey's theory of conversation as based on the premise "that conversation as a fine art depends not upon brilliant speech, but upon a rhetoric of sympathy and association" (introduction, xii). Conversation has a clear place in a system where rhetoric is defined as an imaginative and fanciful exploration of possibility that brings people together, and much of De Quincey's exposition on conversation reflects the perspective he has adopted with respect to rhetoric as a whole. William A. Covino explains this connection: "Prose aspiring to the finest abilities of human discourse bodies forth not a stuffing of thoughtless facts, but the human energy of engagement with an open question, energy seeking a community of intellectual exchange. The model for this searching language, this rhetoric, is conversation" ("Thomas De Quincey" 128). For De Quincey, the recognized value of conversation represents a unique opportunity for demonstrating the social benefits available to individuals who are proficient with language. For De Quincey, conversation serves as one site in which rhetoric carries out its role of infusing public life with intellectual stimulation.

The ostensible purpose of De Quincey's essay is to argue for a more systematic approach to conversation. Woven into this argument is De Quincey's broader view that skillful conversation simultaneously entertains and purposefully strengthens society, a position he establishes in the essay's first sentence: "Amongst the arts connected with the *elegancies* of social life in a degree which nobody denies is the Art of Conversation; but in a degree which almost everybody denies, if one may judge by their neglect of its simple rules, this same art is not less connected with the *uses* of social life" ("Conversation" 264; original emphasis). Given the importance of conversation in maintaining society's strength and stability, De Quincey marvels that conversation has no apparent rules in place, unlike all other arts, even spitting (265). To conceive of conversation as an art is justified, he maintains, because social discourse provides people with opportunities to acquire intellectual power. Noting that Bacon views conversation as the route to reaching one's "possible advantages as a *ready* man," De Quincey argues that skill in conversation actually provides people with an even more significant source of power, for he perceives "an absolute birth of new insight into the truth itself as inseparable from the finer and more scientific exercise of the talking art" (268; original emphasis). Just as the private reflection of rhetoric promotes intellectual stimulation that strengthens both the individual intellect and the public at large, the systematic exercise of private discourse offers a route to knowledge that ultimately benefits society. And conversation has a particular advantage in fulfilling rhetoric's potential to effect social transformation, since it frequently functions as discourse directed toward pleasure and intellectual stimulation rather than being aimed at achieving a specific material objective.

As with other aspects of his rhetorical theory, De Quincey's treatment of conversation both builds on and departs from earlier notions of conversation's rhetorical potential. Cicero provides an early statement of conversation's possible connection to rhetoric in *De officiis*: "The power of speech in the attainment of propriety is great, and its function is twofold: the first is oratory; the second, conversation. . . . There are rules for oratory laid down by rhetoricians; there are none for conversation; and yet I do not know why there should not be. . . . the same rules that we have for words and sentences in rhetoric will apply also to conversation" (1:xxxvii). Bacon's exploration of the subject of friendship includes attention to the intellectual value that conversation among friends provides:

> [C]ertain it is that whosoever hath his mind fraught with many thoughts, his wits and understanding do clarify and break up, in the communicating and discoursing with one another; he tosseth his thoughts more easily; he marshalleth them more orderly; he seeth how they look when they are turned into words: finally, he waxeth wiser than himself; and that more by an hour's discourse than by a day's meditation. (para. 6)

The potential connection between conversation and heightened understanding becomes particularly intriguing for eighteenth-century thinkers.
Jennifer Georgia notes that "the genres of the eighteenth century were
imbued with the social, dialogic rhythm of conversation" (249). The potential for conversation to create a social atmosphere that will promote
constructive intellectual engagement removed from the damaging effects
of modern society is explored in the early eighteenth century by Anthony
Ashley Cooper, Third Earl of Shaftesbury, whose rationale in many respects
anticipates De Quincey's desire to counter the negative effects of modern
society through fanciful discourse that resists immediate resolution. In
Shaftesbury's view, the social accountability preserved in "polite discourse"
provides the ideal setting for reasoned dialogue. Although people innately
possess knowledge of the world and of right conduct, their judgment may
be endangered by excessive appeals to emotion that temporarily overwhelm
the functioning of reason. In defending the wit that he associates with
polite conversation, Shaftesbury insists that people can never be subverted
from their own instinctive regard for the truth when opposing views are
presented with humor and gentility:

> Men indeed may, in a serious way, be so wrought on, and confounded,
> by different Modes of Opinion, different Systems and Schemes *impos'd
> by Authority*, that they may wholly lose all Notion or Comprehension
> of *Truth*. I can easily apprehend what Effect *Awe* has over Mens Un-
> derstandings. I can very well suppose Men may be frighted out of their
> Wits: but I have no apprehension they shou'd be laugh'd out of 'em. I can
> hardly imagine that in a pleasant way they shou'd ever be talk'd out of
> their Love for Society, or reason'd out of Humanity and *common Sense*.
> (60–61; original emphasis)

Conversation also plays a significant role in the moral philosophy of David Hume. According to Amanda Dickins, Hume's belief in conversation
provides a counter to Thomas Hobbes's assumption that opinion inevitably
leads to conflict, as Hume insists that conversation "requires us to see things
from the perspectives of others. . . . Hume's approach postulates a mutual
adjustment of opinion and language: conversation is the medium for this
adjustment and our capacity of sympathy provides both means and motivation" (26). In a similar vein, Adam Smith emphasizes the role of conversation
in preserving the intricate balance between the well-being of the individual
and social harmony in *The Theory of Moral Sentiments*:

Society and conversation, therefore, are the most powerful remedies for restoring the mind to its tranquillity, if, at any time, it has unfortunately lost it; as well as the best preservatives of that equal and happy temper, which is so necessary to self-satisfaction and enjoyment. Men of retirement and speculation, who are apt to sit brooding at home over either grief or resentment, though they may often have more humanity, more generosity, and a nicer sense of honour, yet seldom possess that equality of temper which is so common among men of the world. (1:1:iv.9)

These theorists' suggestions that conversation has value for promoting constructive social interactions, developing the individual's skill with language, and refining the intellect in many respects anticipate De Quincey's view of conversation's capacity to enact a bond between public and private life that will benefit both individuals and their surrounding society.

This benefit originates in the intrinsic link that conversation provides between people. Although De Quincey upholds the value of conversation in promoting true knowledge, he also insists that conversation brings together people with intellectual differences. Like Hume, whose "conversable world" is described by Nancy S. Struever as "the site of serious investigative projects" (239), De Quincey suggests that the intellectual power of conversation is achieved precisely because of its sociable nature: "More will be done for the benefit of conversation by the simple magic of good manners (that is, chiefly by a system of forbearances), applied to the besetting vices of social intercourse, than ever *was* or *can* be done by all varieties of intellectual power assembled upon the same arena" ("Conversation" 266; original emphasis). De Quincey implicitly builds on the eighteenth-century emphasis on sympathy as a central feature of rhetorical practice, describing conversation as the natural site in which the capacity for sympathy is sparked and further developed. Quoting Quintilian's statement that "[t]he heart (and not the brain) is that which makes a man eloquent" ("Conversation" 273), De Quincey insists that conversational ability must be measured according to the speaker's genuine interest in engaging with other people. He argues that Samuel Johnson should not be considered a skillful conversationalist "because he had little interest in man" ("Conversation" 273) and relied instead on conflict as the source of interest in his encounters with others. De Quincey depicts such a conversational approach as sharply contrasting with his own, which conceives of conversation as a sympathetic encounter, the "electric kindling of life between two minds" ("Conversation" 268). He outlines the qualities that formed the basis for his unique talent for conversation at some length in *Confessions*:

Ignorant I was in a degree past all imagination of daily life—even as it exists in England. But, on the other hand, having the advantage of a prodigious memory, and the far greater advantage of a logical instinct for feeling in a moment the secret analogies or parallelisms that connected things else apparently remote, I enjoyed these two peculiar gifts for conversation: first, an inexhaustible fertility of topics, and therefore of resources for illustrating or varying any subject that chance or purpose suggested; secondly, a prematurely awakened sense of *art* applied to conversation. (3:332; original emphasis)

De Quincey's description of his conversational art resonates in interesting ways with the classical canons of invention, arrangement, style, memory, and delivery. In elaborating on his view that conversation is an art, he insists that discussion need not be conceived as disputation. He identifies "two orders" of conversation "*that*, on the one hand, which contemplates an interest of knowledge and of the self-developing intellect; *that*, on the other hand, which forms one and the widest amongst the gay embellishments of life" ("Conversation" 287–88; original emphasis), insisting that the two work together to strengthen social discourse.

Although De Quincey argues that conversation should be conceived as art, he stresses the importance of making conversation appear to be as natural as possible: "It would have been coxcombry to practice any elaborate or any conspicuous art: few and simple were any artifices that I ever employed; but, being hidden and seasonable, they were often effective. And the whole result was, that I became exceedingly popular within my narrow circle of friends" (*Confessions* 3:332–33). He argues for an immediate interaction between conversation and writing, maintaining that the best writers model their prose on the natural flow of conversation. As an example, he cites Burke, whose writings appear to be "governed by the very necessity of growth" ("Conversation" 269) rather than appearing forced to move forward in an obvious and mechanical way. Thus, De Quincey identifies the same strengths in Burke's conversation that he had highlighted in his assessment of Burke's rhetoric, which suggests a complementary relationship between rhetoric and conversation.

De Quincey's success as a conversationalist is somewhat remarkable in light of the fact that he seems to have been somewhat shy, eccentric, and inclined to solitude. His argument for the social success available through conversation, therefore, offers a striking statement about the capacity of artful conversation to establish connections between people. In De Quincey's view, these connections are available because conversation encourages sympathetic encounters that build an intellectual community. De Quincey's perception that rhetoric circulates between the public and private worlds leads him to assign special importance to conversation, which naturally accomplishes a similar objective. He sees books and conversation as existing in a complementary relationship, as conversation can strengthen literary judgment, aid in "the effectual promotion of intellectual culture," and facilitate "the natural integration for the deficiencies of private and sequestered study" ("Conversation" 277). Covino notes that the structure of conversation for De Quincey naturally promotes the process of collective exploration that he advocates: "The individual sentences of colloquial intercourse stay short and simple, but interplay among sentences forms the conversation at large, and we might characterize this larger discourse as a continual sentence of growing, changing theses, couched in the rhythm of the communal mind" ("Thomas De Quincey" 129). Thus, conversation encourages people to engage in a reciprocal relationship that both heightens their individual intellectual powers and contributes to a more harmonious social environment.

In order for these benefits to be realized, De Quincey argues that people will need to be taught to cultivate a new civility in conversation, which will eliminate the "conversational tyranny" that prohibits sympathetic interpersonal engagement and resists the benefits he has outlined ("Conversation" 285). He perceives such tyranny as a trend throughout Western Europe, which "is tending more and more to a mode of living in public" ("Conversation" 285). In a letter to Mrs. Wordsworth, De Quincey describes in detail his visits to the home of his mother's friend Hannah More at Barley Wood, including a vivid depiction of what he considers to be More's unfortunate conversational habits:

> She has described herself sufficiently in her books. . . . [H]er conversation (for that she thinks her forte) is just like them—aphoristic; epigrammatic—nothing been thought to be said well at Barley Wood but what is said pointedly; full of trite quotations—hardly ever introduced to confirm—or illustrate—or because they might adequately convey the feeling—but as cold ornaments and garnishings; or, when she does sometimes make a formal quotation in proof of what she says, it is always—for fear of being thought "a learned lady"—ushered in with an affectation of doubt as to the author—as "I think, it is my lord Bacon who says"—etc. Then everything must be "improved." . . . Moreover she is restless until every thought is brought into such a shape that she can translate it into some of her received positions; and thus every avenue is shut up against

gaining or communicating anything in her company; since, if she finds that the case is desperate and that you will not permit what you say to be lopped down into some of her own previous thoughts, then she makes no further answer but by bowing her head. (qtd. in Sackville-West 115–16)

Thus, in conversation, as in rhetoric more generally, De Quincey emphasizes the need to allow thoughts to range freely, a process that naturally draws people together in an exploratory manner. Those who are determined to bring discourse to a hasty or predetermined conclusion, using forms of discourse that "take the listener for a person who passively understands but not for one who actively answers and reacts" (Bakhtin, "Discourse" 280), are circumventing rhetoric's power to foster genuine critical inquiry.

De Quincey's conviction that conversation must be a reciprocal endeavor leads him to question social conventions that interfere with this pursuit. His reflections about his encounter with King George III during his youth center upon these questions: "Could it be likely that much truth of a general nature, bearing upon man and social interests, could ever reach the ear of a king, under the etiquette of a court, and under that one rule which seemed singly sufficient to foreclose all natural avenues to truth—the rule, I mean, by which it is forbidden to address a question to the King" ("I Enter the World" 1:171). He goes on to argue that this convention deprives the king of the opportunity to achieve the full range of intellectual development since it forces him to maintain entire control of the conversation:

But what becomes of that man's general condition of mind in relation to all the great objects moving on the field of human experience, where it is a law generally for almost all who approach him, that they shall confine themselves to replies, absolute responses, or, at most, to a prosecution of carrying forward of a proposition delivered by the *protagonist*, or supreme leader of the conversation? For it must be remembered that, generally speaking, the effect of putting no question is to transfer into the other party's hands the entire *originating* movement of the dialogue; and thus, in a musical metaphor, the great man is the sole modulator and determiner of the key in which the conversation proceeds. ("I Enter the World" 1:172; original emphasis)

Thus, in spite of De Quincey's Tory leanings, his strong commitment to conversation as a shared inquiry prompts him to suggest that the form of respect that limits the subjects' rights to free interaction with the king might actually be intellectually debilitating for both parties.

De Quincey further articulates the hazards of neglecting the principles of a truly dialogic conversation in a passage in *Confessions* that begins with the deficiencies of vapid conversation and concludes with a discussion of Coleridge's practice of conversational dominance:

> Come from what fountain it may, all talk that succeeds to the extent of raising a wish to meet the talker again, must contain *salt*; must be seasoned with some flavouring element pungent enough to neutralize the natural tendencies of all mixed conversation, not vigilantly tended, to lose itself in insipidities and platitudes. Above all things, I shunned, as I would shun a pestilence, Coleridge's capital error, which through life he practised, of keeping the audience in a state of passiveness. Unjust this was to others, but most of all to himself. This eternal stream of talk which never for one instant intermitted, and allowed no momentary opportunity of reaction to the persecuted and bated auditor was absolute ruin to the interests of the talker himself. Always passive—always acted upon, never allowed to react, into what state did the poor afflicted listener—he that played the *role* of listener—collapse? He returned home in the exhausted condition of one that has been drawn up just before death from the bottom of a well occupied by foul gases; and, of course, hours before he had reached that perilous point of depression, he had lost all power of distinguishing, understanding, or connecting. (3:331–32; original emphasis)

To cause listeners to experience the sensation of those who have resided at "the bottom of a well occupied by foul gases" is clearly evidence of what De Quincey describes as "unamiable arrogance" that reveals "principles of deadliest selfishness" (3:332). He goes on to suggest that to allow such an attitude to go unchecked not only diminishes the speaker's credibility and ability to establish connections with others but also entails "incapacitating my hearer from doing any justice to the rhetoric or the argument with which I might address him" (3:332). In contrast with Coleridge's practice of arrogantly ignoring the needs of those with whom he converses, De Quincey offers a theory of artful conversation that fosters sympathetic connection with others and provides a forum in which people may share their perspectives with each other, a process compatible with sound rhetorical practice.

In De Quincey's view, the conditions of modern life have posed challenges for conversation as well as rhetorical practice more generally, but he argues that these conditions obligate people to seek modes of conversing that foster greater sympathetic interaction. He notes that just as the increased use of public rooms eventually led to more careful regulations in their use, the increase in public interaction should lead to agreement about the principles that govern the way people converse with each other. He whimsically suggests that such principles might include an accepted method for preventing one person from dominating conversation, such as a time-keeping device similar to that used in Roman courts, to intervene in cases where a speaker holds forth without a proper sense of timing, or that designated leaders could be assigned the task of ensuring that conversations move forward appropriately rather than drifting into areas that lack interest for any of the participants. In addition, he argues for the development of a conversational style "fitted for a purpose which is one of pure enjoyment" ("Conversation" 287), which will necessarily involve more efficient use of language.

De Quincey's suggestions for regulating conversation are offered in a somewhat humorous vein, and some of his criticisms of Coleridge's conversational tyranny likely serve a personal agenda distinct from his argument for conversational principles that will benefit the public at large. However, his belief in the importance of conversation reflects his broader commitment to exploring language's role in strengthening society. De Quincey's view of conversation as "a powerful ally of education and generally of self-culture" can be seen as an outgrowth of his vision of rhetorical discourse, which circulates between the individual's internal thought processes and broader public concerns. Conversation provides one means of encouraging people to develop strategies for rhetorically negotiating the divide between themselves and others, developing a dialogic consciousness that can ultimately benefit society as a whole. In *Dialogue, Dialectic, and Conversation: A Social Perspective on the Function of Writing*, Gregory Clark articulates connections among conversation, writing, and rhetoric: "Because, according to general conversation theory, people use the exchange that term describes to define the common meanings, the shared knowledge, upon which they can build their future cooperation, it seems that most conversations, at some level of their social function, are, as Farrell uses the term, rhetorical" (39). De Quincey perceives conversation as a way to establish this type of cooperative understanding, the means by which individuals arrive at new insights through openly engaging with others' perspectives. Don H. Bialostosky explains that in dialogic conversation, "Those who take their turns speaking and listening, representing others and being represented by them, learn not just who these others are but who they themselves may be, not just what others may mean but what they themselves may mean among others" ("Dialogics" 792). The process of inquiry that allows people to arrive at new insights about "what they themselves may mean among others"

(Bialostosky, "Dialogics" 792) lies at the heart of De Quincey's rhetoric. The art of conversation represents one avenue through which De Quincey seeks to promote the creative intellectual discipline that he conceives to be a necessary component in rhetoric's revitalization.

De Quincey's Eddying Thoughts upon Rhetoric

At first glance, De Quincey's prescription for rhetoric's revitalization might appear to call for its complete retreat into the rarefied realm of individual subjectivity. However, De Quincey avoids defining the intellectual play involved in rhetoric in terms that separate individuals entirely from the concerns of the external world. His historical investigation consistently assumes that language both responds to and shapes the society in which it is situated, as is evident in his statement that contemporary critics must recognize that Demosthenes's style reflects "the composition of his audience" ("Brief Appraisal" 329). In fact, this for De Quincey is where rhetoric's challenge lies. If rhetoric's potential could be realized purely through the agency of individual genius, it would not be so severely affected by social environments hostile to the leisurely exploration of ideas. A central challenge for rhetoric in modern life within De Quincey's system lies in his insistence that public concerns provide the catalyst for rhetoric, even as true rhetorical practice moves beyond a concern with the resolution of specific issues. De Quincey sees rhetoric as firmly embedded in public life, as individuals receive inspiration to practice rhetoric through their engagement with the external world and in turn stimulate public thought through their rhetorical practice. However, De Quincey's deliberate departure from earlier assumptions about rhetoric's integral role in resolving civic issues helps to set the stage for rhetoric's nineteenth-century transformation from direct engagement with civic questions to an appropriation of rhetoric in support of an indirect transformation of society through a disinterested response that is open to several possible interpretations.

Thus, De Quincey's emphasis on rhetorical subjectivity over factual discourse is accompanied by a resistance to any notion of rhetoric that resides solely in the individual's internal consciousness. Although he does insist the writer's task is "to project his own inner mind" ("Style" 226), De Quincey's view of a productive projection of the inner mind does not involve a retreat into concerns that are strictly private, since such a retreat would prevent the dialogic energy that comes from exploring multiple positions. In spite of his deep reverence for Wordsworth, his complaint about the poet's "one-sidedness" ("Gradual Estrangement" 3:204) establishes a contrast between De Quincey's view of rhetoric and the constraints that operate in poetic genres, which Bakhtin depicts as prevented from attaining a dialogic perspective due to the need for artistic unity:

> In poetic genres, artistic consciousness—understood as a unity of all the author's semantic and expressive intentions—fully realizes itself within its own language; in them alone is such consciousness fully immanent, expressing itself in it directly and without mediation, without conditions and without distance. The language of the poet is *his* language, he is utterly immersed in it, inseparable from it, he makes use of each form, each word, each expression according to its unmediated power to assign meaning . . . that is, as a pure and direct expression of his own intention. ("Discourse" 285; original emphasis)

De Quincey's resistance to rhetoric deriving from "a pure and direct expression" of the writer's perspective is evident in his critique of Sir Philip Francis, whom he dismisses as a rhetorician on the grounds that "not in a solitary instance did his barren understanding ascend to an abstraction or general idea, but lingered for ever in the dust and rubbish of individuality" ("Rhetoric" 119). His negative assessment of John Milton's rhetorical aptitude has a similar basis, as he notes that, with the exception of "Areopagitica," Milton fails to produce prose works "upon a theme of universal interest, or perhaps fitted to be the ground-work of a rhetorical display" ("Rhetoric" 102). His discussion of Greek and Roman rhetoricians in "Brief Appraisal of Greek Literature" is punctuated with observations about the necessity of external stimulation that offers the rhetorician opportunities for new insight. He acknowledges Isocrates's interest in public affairs but blames what he characterizes as Isocrates's "languid" oratory on limitations that derive from his existence as a teacher rather than practitioner of rhetoric, arguing for "the superiority, even for artificial ornaments, of downright practical business and the realities of political strife over the atmosphere of a study or a school" ("Brief Appraisal" 324). In contrast, De Quincey maintains that "in Cicero all habits and all practices were nursed by the daily practice of life and its impassioned realities in the forum or in the senate. . . . Such are the advantages from real campaigns, from the unsimulated strife of actual stormy life, over the torpid dreams of what the Romans called an *umbratic* experience" ("Brief Appraisal" 324; original emphasis). For De Quincey, rhetoric must not be entirely focused on resolving practical affairs, but it also cannot thrive if it is entirely removed from a consideration of issues that are of importance in social life.

De Quincey's desire to infuse public discourse with the vitality of the individual's creativity reflects his perception of a cultural shift that was beginning to replace personal authenticity with the mass market. In part, this cultural change is connected with the rise of print, as De Quincey himself suggests. Michael Warner argues that in eighteenth-century American culture, "the imaginary reference point of the public was constructed through an understanding of print" (162). According to Warner, print is central to a republican culture in which individual citizens are asked to subsume their personal desire to an unstated public good: "It was in the culture of republicanism, with its categories of disinterested virtue and supervision, that a rhetoric of print consumption became authoritative, a way of understanding the publicness of publication" (163). Warner explains that the rise of periodicals such as the *Spectator* enacts a detached public persona that is determined to be the cultural ideal, "[b]ut it could not come about without a value placed on the anonymity here associated with print" (163). In this way, Warner maintains, writing in the eighteenth century comes "to perform the disincorporation of its authors and its readers" (164).

Certainly, De Quincey's writing reveals his sensitivity to the dangers associated with disembodied prose and his determination to define rhetoric in ways that would combat this tendency. His offhand reference to "the elegant but desultory Blair" ("Style" 192) signals his intention to design a rhetorical approach that recaptures the intensity lost through eighteenth-century views of language and an orderly society. In his *Confessions*, he elaborates on his sense that a culture of politeness has overwhelmed individual expression of identity: "So thick a curtain of *manners* is drawn over the features and expression of men's natures, that, to the ordinary observer, the two extremities, and the infinite field of varieties which lie between them, are all confounded under one neutral disguise" (3:369; original emphasis). De Quincey, clearly, conceives it as rhetoric's task to strip away the disguises that have sacrificed individual expression to the social forms that have ultimately encouraged sameness and intellectual mediocrity.

De Quincey's Romantic insistence upon the individual's subjective vision can also be seen as a response to the cultural value placed on facts due to the rise of science, business, and journalism. In taking note of the intrusion of journalistic facts in nineteenth-century literary production, Christopher A. Kent discusses at some length the example of author Charles Reade, whose "strange thralldom to journalism was closely related to his literalist realism and his distrust of creativity" (7). Certainly, De Quincey's insistence upon the validity of the creative vision of the inspired individual can be seen as a counter to what Kent describes as a "literary version of naïve empiricism—that, just as the progress of science is the automatic consequence of the accumulation of factual information about the world, so too the progress of literature depends on the increased accumulation of verified incidents" (7). His theories concerning rhetoric are aimed at offering a method of developing intellectual vitality through the dialogic engagement with possibilities unavailable in the world of scientific fact, in keeping with what Raymond Williams describes as Romanticism's "alternative construction of human motive and energy, in contrast with the assumptions of the prevailing political economy" (42).

Thus, De Quincey identifies rhetoric as a dialogic use of language that offers an imaginative alternative to the demand for factual certainty that dominated nineteenth-century public discourse. De Quincey's rhetoric serves as an example of what Bialostosky identifies as a Wordsworthian strain of dialogism, whose aim is "to discover a radical alternative version of the world in dialogic competition with 'common sense'" (*Wordsworth* 223). This dialogic competition entails an engagement with possibility that places De Quincey's rhetoric at the intersection of public and private life, as he insists that rhetoricians must maintain an interest in public life without becoming so absorbed in it that they fail to allow their individual gifts with language to come to full development. Such development requires patience and a willingness to devote time to internal deliberation—a process that goes against modern trends. De Quincey's subtle distinctions among rhetorical introspection and sentimentality, social stimulation and "a vulgar scuffle for power" ("Rhetoric" 121), and the "rubbish of individuality" and the rhetorical benefit of the "eddying about" of one's thoughts contribute to a complex definition of rhetoric that maintains dialectical tensions that at times appear contradictory. In elaborating on the complicated balances rhetoric requires—between public and private, fanciful and disciplined— De Quincey exemplifies the playful discipline he perceives to lie at the heart of rhetorical practice—and demonstrates the "motion of fancy self-sustained from its own activities" that he perceives as the key to intellectual and social vitality.

CHAPTER 4

De Quincey's "Science of Style"

A s the previous chapter argues, De Quincey responds to what he perceives as a decline in the intellectual energy of nineteenth-century
society with an argument for rhetoric's capacity to revitalize public life
through facilitating a free and imaginative exploration of the individual's
subjectivity. His Romantic view that intellectual vitality develops through
an encounter with possibility leads him to the conviction that rhetoric
must involve a dialogic engagement with varied perspectives. He strategically appropriates Aristotelian rhetoric, arguably the exemplar of rhetorical
practicality, to revise rhetorical history, as he insists that true rhetoric has
always entailed the use of language to investigate multiple alternatives. In
De Quincey's hands, the emphasis of rhetoric shifts from arriving at judgment about urgent political questions to a process through which individuals investigate matters of probability, an enterprise that fosters intellectual
growth. He insists that the emphasis placed on the immediate resolution of
specific issues by science and business has stifled the creative impulse that
constitutes rhetoric's strength. Thus, De Quincey maintains a public role
for rhetoric, but that role emerges through the expansive mental activity
of individuals willing to commit themselves to the disciplined yet fanciful
language use that can challenge the intellectual malaise of modern society.

De Quincey's emphasis on the individual's intellectual process over the
practical outcome of a specific argument significantly elevates the role of
style in rhetorical activity. This emphasis on style can be seen as a typical
feature of dialogic rhetoric, a point that Charles I. Schuster emphasizes in
exploring the implications of Bakhtinian dialogism for rhetoric: "Bakhtin's
paradigm leads us toward aesthetic concerns in language. Bakhtin is most
concerned with sophisticated language use, with forms that convey multiple
orientations and interpretations" (8). De Quincey anticipates Bakhtin in
recognizing the role of style in supporting the imaginative investigation of
alternative possibilities.

As is the case with his approach to rhetoric more generally, De Quincey's emphasis on style does not constitute a complete departure from earlier strains in the British rhetorical tradition. Thomas Wilson's *Arte of Rhetorique* (1553), the first complete rhetorical treatise written in English, places a strong emphasis on style as the means to acquire *ethos* (Agnew, "Rhetorical Style"). The numerous British manuals following Wilson's treatise, such as Richard Sherry's *Treatise of Schemes and Tropes* (1550) and Henry Peacham's *Garden of Eloquence* (1577), attest to the emphasis on style among British rhetorics at the end of that century. The seventeenth century's pursuit of a plain style suited to the needs of the scientific community illustrates the continued assumption that styles of communication play an integral role in rhetoric's imperative to respond to changing purposes and audiences. Numerous innovations in eighteenth-century British rhetorics sustain the long-standing attention to style among British language theorists, including George Campbell's emphasis on vivacity and attention to usage, extensive treatments of taste most famously exemplified in Hugh Blair's *Lectures on Rhetoric and Belles Lettres*, and the preoccupation with propriety found in numerous eighteenth-century British rhetorical treatises. Long before De Quincey, British rhetorical theorists had in various ways developed arguments concerning the significant role of style in rhetorical proficiency and civic vitality.

Like his view of rhetoric, then, De Quincey's discussion of style both builds on and transforms earlier theories. I have previously argued that even his 1828 discussion of rhetoric features a critical engagement with ideas that can be seen as a type of persuasion that has some connection with earlier iterations of rhetoric, but his treatment of style perhaps more clearly accommodates traditional views of rhetoric's function. Although Frederick Haberman argues that De Quincey's 1828 essay ignores the question of audience in a way that appears to assume that "rhetoric is a game of solitaire," he describes De Quincey's discussion of style, in contrast, as acknowledging "the audience as a central figure in the composition. Rhetoric here is persuasion; it is a practical art" (198). Indeed, De Quincey's initial description of style as "the ministerial part of Rhetoric" seems to follow a fairly standard pattern of reasoning, as he observes that "any arts which conciliate regard to the speaker indirectly promote the effect of his argument" ("Rhetoric" 92). In this passage, De Quincey appears to emphasize the relationship between style and ethos in much the same way that his predecessors across several centuries of British rhetoric's development had done.

However, De Quincey insists even more emphatically than many of his rhetorical forebears that style plays an integral role in rhetorical invention due to the strong connection, he assumes, between rhetoric and the writer's subjectivity. In part, this assumption reflects De Quincey's Romantic tendencies. Rex Veeder argues that a key principle of British Romantic rhetoric is that "the purpose of education is to negotiate between private and public discourse in order to create a personal ethos capable of interacting with dynamic social change" ("Expressive Rhetoric" 102). For Romantics, the conditions of modern life required an emphasis on personal subjectivity that could counter the social fragmentation and mechanism that accompanied industrialization. Veeder goes on to explain that in response to these conditions, the Romantic "emphasis on character engendered an accent on style and voice in writing" ("Expressive Rhetoric" 102), which leads to a view of ethos that differs from that found in many of De Quincey's predecessors in the British rhetorical tradition. Referencing Lionel Trilling, Jason Camlot states that "the trajectory of nineteenth-century rhetoric and critical theory moves from a socially implicated, rhetorically informed discourse of sincerity, towards the idea of an immediately transparent, self-evident being, manifested as autonomous and authentic" (3). This shift parallels S. Michael Halloran's argument that the classical assumption that the orator's task entails speaking "the word of communal wisdom" (79) is replaced in modern rhetoric with the view that the defining character of ethos resides in the "responsibility of the speaker (or author) to articulate his own world, and thereby his own self" (89). These assessments that rhetoric's evolution gradually leads to an emphasis not on the objective criteria that determine rhetorical success but on the internal manifestation of an individual's thought processes is very much in keeping with De Quincey's vision of rhetorical and stylistic success.

At the same time, his vision of self-discovery that entails a playful engagement with shifting perspectives and paradoxes departs from what might appear to be a straightforward endorsement of self-expression as an outpouring of the individual's internal impressions. In discussing the significance of Bakhtin for a renewed emphasis on style in composition, Schuster articulates the connections among style, subjectivity, and multiple possibilities in a dialogic rhetoric: "Bakhtin argues that style *is* language, that to create a style is to create a language for oneself. . . . Furthermore, to attend to style in language is, according to Bakhtin, to perceive the interpretive richness of discourse" (4; original emphasis). In advocating style as the mechanism for both self-expression and intellectual discovery, De Quincey's articulation of a rhetoric defined by the creative energy of the individual builds upon but significantly revises earlier assumptions about style as a component of the rhetor's ethos and enacts a Romantic vision that stresses the dialogic use of language that moves beyond the individual's existing knowledge in order to discover new possibilities.

De Quincey explains his views about style and its importance in an essay titled "Style," published in four installments of *Tait's Magazine* between 1840 and 1841. As the previous chapter notes, De Quincey's literary and rhetorical theory did not receive as much attention at the time of its publication as his autobiographical essays. However, both Julian North and H. O. Dendurent find some interest in De Quincey's theory of style in the decades following the essay's publication. Although Dendurent's annotation of George Saintsbury's review of De Quincey's work in his 1904 *History of Criticism* highlights Saintsbury's generally negative assessment of De Quincey, Dendurent relates Saintsbury's view that "Rhetoric" and "Style" reflect that De Quincey is "a fine preceptist critic" (70). North comments that David Masson describes De Quincey's essays "Rhetoric," "Style," and "Language" as having "superseded Addison, Johnson, Jeffrey, and Whately" (*De Quincey Reviewed* 122). De Quincey's contribution to contemporary conversations about style met with some approval even by those who otherwise tended to denigrate his theoretical work.

The form of De Quincey's essay differs substantially from previous treatments of style among rhetorical theorists. As Camlot explains in his chapter on De Quincey, "De Quincey's essay on style does not function as a manual of style . . . but as a history of style with the purpose of explaining the actual conditions under which the best kind of un-mechanical prose style can arise" (85). This consideration begins with De Quincey's assessment of the problematic tendency to divide style and content. In "Rhetoric," De Quincey notes that the inadequate understanding of rhetoric that can be observed throughout its history has derived from a false opposition between decorative language, which had often been associated with sophistry, and the argument's substance (82). He elaborates on this point in "Style," where he charges the British public with a confused attitude toward style that has had negative consequences for language use and, consequently, the nation's intellectual strength. He identifies confusion about style as one of "three aspects there are of our national character which trouble the uniformity of our feelings" ("Style" 134) and explains that this confusion "tends in all things to set the matter above the manner, the substance above the external show,—a principle noble in itself, but inevitably wrong wherever the manner blends inseparably with the substance" ("Style" 137). De Quincey's essay offers a vision of style as inextricably linked to invention, an approach tied to his view of rhetoric's central role in promoting creative energy and intellectual engagement with language. In discussing the link De Quincey creates between invention and style, Hoyt H. Hudson argues, "The mode of thinking which is rhetorical invention demands a methodology of inference different from that of rigorously logical thinking" (205). In De Quincey's view, to recognize the unity of matter and manner, style and substance enables people to restore rhetoric's capacity to manifest the individual's creative exploration of ideas.

This assumption guides De Quincey's view that style is best developed in writings that are primarily subjective, since too great an absorption in external concerns tends to obscure the writer's awareness of the integral role of language in communicating thought. Following his investigation of the development of style in different historical periods and cultures, De Quincey concludes that influences common to ancient Greece and the Medieval period contribute to the proper cultivation of style: "1. The same condition of intellect under revolutionary excitement; 2. The same penury of books; 3. The same chilling gloom from the absence of female charities . . . ; 4. The same . . . enthusiasm and elevation of thought from disinterested participation in forwarding a great movement of the age" ("Style" 226). According to De Quincey, such influences inevitably lead people to develop a focus on subjectivity that is "peculiarly favourable to the culture of style" (226). In keeping with Coleridge's argument that "the best part of human language, properly so called, is derived from reflection on the acts of the mind itself" (*Biographia Literaria* 197), De Quincey explains that while meticulous attention to style is almost inevitable for those who are detached from external concerns, careless language use is more common in "[a] man who has absolute facts to communicate from some branch of study external to himself" ("Style 226). De Quincey notes that "[p]onderable facts and external realities are intelligible in almost any language; they are self-explained and self-sustained" ("Style" 229), but goes on to add that

> the more closely any exercise of mind is connected with what is internal and individual in the sensibilities,—that is, with what is philosophically termed *subjective*,—precisely in that degree, and the more subtly, does the style or the embodying of the thoughts cease to be a mere separable ornament, and in fact the more does the manner, as we expressed it before, become confluent with the matter. ("Style" 229; original emphasis)

De Quincey, therefore, aligns himself with Wordsworth in describing language as "the *incarnation* of thoughts" ("Style" 230; original emphasis)—an incarnation that can only be fully realized when those thoughts are allowed to roam freely without too much interference from the world of facts.

In his essay titled "Oxford," De Quincey offers a two-part definition of the components of style, the coherence of thought and the relationships among sentences:

> The two capital secrets in the art of prose composition are these: 1st, The philosophy of transition and connection, or the art by which one step in an evolution of thought is made to arise out of another: all fluent and effective composition depends on the *connections*;—2dly, The way in which sentences are made to modify each other; for the most powerful effects in written eloquence arise out of this reverberation, as it were, from each other in a rapid succession of sentences; and, because some limitation is necessary to the length and complexity of sentences, in order to make this interdependency felt. (2:65; original emphasis)

For De Quincey, the art of style facilitates the connections and modifications that are integral to the development of complex ideas. This relationship establishes style's central role in De Quincey's rhetoric, which is based on an intensive exploration of ideas rather than the outcome of a persuasive exchange.

De Quincey's emphasis on rhetorical subjectivity, therefore, establishes the parameters within which style's persuasive work takes place. He argues that "all subjective branches of study favour the cultivation of style" ("Style" 229), for style has an important part in the writer's task, which is "to project his own inner mind" (226). However, De Quincey does not conceive of the writer's "inner mind" as a static entity but instead imagines that mind as one that engages freely with multiple perspectives. The internal function of style ensures its place in intellectual development; through its role in manifesting connections among thoughts, style serves as a resource that helps the writer develop ideas in the disciplined and productive manner that De Quincey believes to be necessary in order for true creativity to flourish.

Although style should offer writers a framework that illuminates the significance of ideas as they develop, the parameters of rhetorical style should not be restricted by practical demands for efficiency. De Quincey emphasizes rhetoric that exemplifies discipline and a focused purpose, but his commitment to creativity and intellectual play as central features of rhetoric challenges the emphases on conciseness and coherence that were emerging as key components of good style in the nineteenth century. De Quincey assumes that rhetoricians involved in "eddying about their own thoughts"

("Rhetoric" 121) do sustain a line of thought that is in some measure connected and ultimately promotes forces that "may activate and organize" ideas (Bakhtin, "Discourse" 277). At the same time, he perceives the need to allow rhetorical insights to emerge through creative processes that are not as straightforward as the writers of nineteenth-century rhetorical handbooks would suggest. De Quincey conceives of the subjective exploration of thought as an active process that entails engagement with multiple perspectives, a strict rejection of what Bakhtin describes as the "passive understanding" of language that emphasizes the practical requirements of communication ("Discourse" 281). For De Quincey, the best type of language use entails the complex discovery of unity in the midst of apparent fragmentation, a process that reflects the nature of human experience. In "The Affliction of Childhood," he writes, "Man is doubtless *one* by some subtle *nexus*, some system of links, that we cannot perceive, extending from the new-born infant to the superannuated dotard: but, as regards many affections and passions incident to his nature at different stages, he is *not* one, but an intermitting creature, ending and beginning anew; the unity of man, in this respect, is co-extensive only with the particular stage to which the passion belongs" (1:43; original emphasis). De Quincey's belief in the malleable nature of human life, combined with his sense of rhetoric as a dynamic reflection of human subjectivity, leads him to shift the focus of rhetoric from coherence to strategic intellectual play that captures the "intermitting" quality of human experience, an idea he sustains in his essay on rhetoric and in his own writings.

De Quincey maintains that the significance of this disciplined play with language leads to style that is not, as the English have tended to imagine, "a mere ornamental accident of written composition—a trivial embellishment" but is instead both substantial and intellectually rigorous, "a product of art the rarest, subtlest, and most intellectual; and, like other products of the fine arts, it is then finest when it is most eminently disinterested—that is, most conspicuously detached from gross palpable uses" ("Style" 261). Although De Quincey links style to invention in ways that take the audience into account, his focus on industrial society's detrimental effect on rhetoric and his determination that rhetoric entails the expansive exploration of ideas lead him to insist that the proper cultivation of style must include a detachment from practical concerns, a point that anticipates the focus on disinterestedness advocated later in the nineteenth century by theorists such as Matthew Arnold and Walter Pater.

De Quincey's insistence that style is "finest when it is most eminently disinterested" again emphasizes his view that the appreciation for creative expression is consistently threatened by an emphasis on language's practical function that curtails the free exploration of ideas through language. In De Quincey's view, a focus on language's instrumental function imposes limits on the process of discovery that should lie at the heart of the rhetorical enterprise. His fusion of style and invention contributes to his assumption that the manner in which ideas are expressed has a direct relationship to the strength of the ideas themselves. Paul M. Talley takes note of the fact that De Quincey's treatment of "the origin and development of prose as the form of public discourse . . . quickly modulates into its major theme, which is that the form of discourse imposes control upon the thought in the discourse" (251). Camlot describes De Quincey's discussion of style as engaged "in dialogue" with Wordsworth's concern about the harmful effects of publication, adding, "Where for Wordsworth, the problem was not in the conception of the grand thoughts, but in their publication and reception, for De Quincey, all three problems are substantial, and the establishment of the best conditions under which grand thoughts can arise is especially pressing" (85). De Quincey identifies the English insistency upon practicality as a major factor in the evolution of conditions that have not been favorable to the articulation of complex ideas, which has a reciprocal effect on social values. He notes that "the right of occupying the attention of the company seems to inhere in *things* rather than in persons; if the particular subject under discussion should happen to be a grave one, then, in right of *that,* and not by any right of his own, a speaker will seem to an Englishman invested with the privilege of drawing largely upon the attention of a company" ("Style" 156–57; original emphasis). In contrast, for the French, "this right of participation in the talk is a *personal* right, which cannot be set aside by any possible claims in the subject; it passes by necessity to and fro, backwards and forwards, between the several persons who are present" ("Style" 157; original emphasis). Thus, the French provide a positive example of style grounded in the shared investigation of ideas rather than a straightforward explication of facts, as the collective right to engage with ideas becomes the basis for communication that is dynamic and varied. On the other hand, the English belief that the value of discourse derives from its matter has limited the expansive potential of English style, which, in turn, has contributed to a contemporary tendency to destroy rhetoric through restricting people's opportunities to engage freely in the realm of ideas.

De Quincey describes this trend as one that does not necessarily reflect the English audience's inability to value proficiency with language. He cites the general appreciation for popular eloquence as an indication that the English public attends to skillful language use, but he laments that people are not more inclined to pursue a deeper understanding of the specific qualities in language that appeal to them ("Style" 138–39). The failure to inquire more thoroughly into the workings of language can be seen as the result of a general lack of interest in style, due to the view that style is less significant than the more immediately useful and, therefore, highly valued substance that is communicated. De Quincey insists that this view is mistaken, offering a numerical list of reasons for coming to new insight into the value of style. He begins with the premise that even those who attribute to style the most mechanical function are aware of its ability to offer "intellectual pleasure" (260). Moreover, he notes that placing style in service to the subject of discourse should still entail some appreciation for the role of style in clarifying and enlivening a subject (260). De Quincey then insists that the most serious failure in the English inattention to style relates to a third and more profound perspective, "where style cannot be regarded as a *dress* or alien covering, but where style becomes the *incarnation* of the thoughts. . . . Imagery is sometimes not the mere alien appareling of a thought, and of a nature to be detached from the thought, but is the coefficient that, being superadded to something else, absolutely *makes* the thought as a *third* and separate existence" ("Style" 262; original emphasis). Lacking an awareness of style's capacity to generate thought seriously hampers the vitality of language and its capacity to play an active role in refining the public intellect. What is needed, then, is a more conscious attention to style, a more thorough appreciation for its importance, and an awareness of the distinct demands surrounding oral and written style, the latter of which serves as a particular focus of De Quincey's essay.

De Quincey draws upon history to support his view that an awareness of style comes about through cultivating an appreciation for its substantive role in discourse. While De Quincey admits that the Greeks had some proficiency in rhetoric, he maintains that their view of rhetoric's competitive nature prevented them from acquiring a "full expanded consciousness of the separate idea expressed by *style*" ("Style" 190; original emphasis). He argues that the Roman appreciation for style was somewhat more complete but still deficient. De Quincey proposes to develop a system that can do away with the barriers that might prevent people from acquiring a sense of style, offering "*practical* suggestions" that will "apply to the mechanology of style" (191; original emphasis). He insists that this focus on specific components of style can create a systematic approach that will replace the confusing array of contemporary rhetorical theorists, including the French belletrists and "the elegant, but desultory Blair" (192), with a "systematic art, as regular a subject for training and mechanic discipline, as the science of discrete quantity in Arithmetic, or of continuous quantity in Geometry" (192). While this highly technical approach might seem at odds with De Quincey's emphasis on infusing rhetoric with the individual's creative energy, he claims that his approach will not lead to standardization: "[I]f a mechanic system of training for style would have the same leveling effects as these false calig-raphies, better by far that we should retain our old ignorance. If art is to terminate in a killing monotony, welcome the old condition of inartificial simplicity!" (193). De Quincey's certainty that creating a more methodical system of style will not lead to sameness derives from his conviction that the essence of style cannot be fully mechanized, even as he insists that style should be made more systematic to the extent that this is possible. His discussion of style is, therefore, meant to heighten awareness of style and provide principles for acquiring the discipline that will ultimately contribute to a more unrestrained outpouring of the individual's creative energy. His conviction that style can combine creative energy with system leads him to resist what he sees as the "desultory" stylistic guidance of belletrists such as Blair, on one hand, and the mechanical efficiency of the style expected by the English reading public, on the other.

De Quincey's System: The Mechanology and Organology of Style

This discipline involves acquiring control over a complicated language sys-tem. De Quincey notes that most studies of style simply provide catalogues of specific problems without adequate attention to the broader principles that determine how language is used. He identifies two components of style: the organic and the mechanic. The mechanic emphasizes grammatical structures, possessing what De Quincey describes as a "narrow meaning, expressing the mere *synthesis onomaton*, the syntaxis or combinations of words into sentences" ("Style" 163). Organic style, which Camlot describes as "very close to the romantic theory of language that Mill inherited from Wordsworth" (84), is "of far wider extent, and expressing all possible rela-tions that can arise between thoughts and words—the total effect of a writer as derived from manner" (De Quincey, "Style" 163). De Quincey notes that just as the human body is sustained by the harmonious working of a complex organic system and is "exercised as a machine . . . subject to the laws of motion and equilibrium" ("Style" 164), the language that expresses human thought may be seen as both organic and mechanical. Thus, the "science of style" can be defined both as "organology," examining style as an "organ of thought" and "mechanology," which considers the workings of style through examining how "words act upon words, and through a particular grammar" ("Style" 164). De Quincey sets out to attend to both branches of this science, demonstrating his conviction of the importance of the way all aspects of language use affect the ideas that are expressed. At the same time, Camlot argues that "at the crux of De Quincey's rhetorical theory is the fear that the organic and mechanic modes of style will be confused or elided. . . . De Quincey's assertion of the organic as a distinct rhetorical model represents one strategy by which to protect language from the discursive jargon of periodical prose" (84).

De Quincey's chief focus in the mechanical area rests on the periodic style, which he describes as the source of "downright physical exhaustion" deriving from the lengthy period of anticipation before the "coming round of the sentence commences" ("Style" 158). De Quincey's complaint about the periodic style is interesting in light of his definition of rhetoric as "eddying about" ("Rhetoric" 121) the thoughts. Although this might initially appear to be a contradiction, further reflection suggests that the two principles can actually be seen as supporting each other. De Quincey's willingness to indulge in digression and expansive exploration of ideas is balanced by his insistence that individual sentences provide the reader with a clear sense of purpose. To force readers to exert themselves to follow the development of each sentence would potentially jeopardize their attention to the development of the entire passage. He expresses the fear that readers will in fact lose all interest in following the development of ideas when so much of their attention must be devoted to the meaning of each sentence, as "the continued repetition of so Atlantean an effort soon overwhelms your patience, and establishes at length that habitual feeling which causes you to shrink from the speculations of journalists, or (which is more likely) to adopt a worse habit than absolute neglect" ("Style" 159). De Quincey insists that attention to sentence length and structure will energize both writers and readers and allow for the development of style that more fully supports the exploration of complex ideas.

Thus, De Quincey shares Wordsworth's emphasis on the importance of "the natural order and connection of the words" (qtd. in Heffernan 39), as he emphasizes mechanical structures that support the organic relationships among ideas that lie at the heart of language. This view also parallels that of Coleridge, whom Jerome Christensen describes as emphasizing in *The Friend* the capacity of language to foster relationships: "What becomes natural to the man of superior mind is to be able to traverse a network of relations (between himself and things, things themselves, things and his hearers) that is the discourse by which he is recognized and in which he comes to recognize himself—not only the occasionally fragmentary self that appears but the whole self that he then intends to communicate" (13). De Quincey recognizes that sustaining these intellectual relationships requires attention to words and sentences and the methodical construction of paragraphs at the sentence level. In "Language," he argues,

> A sentence, even when insulated and viewed apart for itself, is a subject for complex art: even *so* far it is capable of multiform beauty, and liable to a whole *nosology* of malconformations. But it is in the *relation* of sentences, in what Horace terms their "*junctura*," that the true life of composition resides. The mode of their *nexus*, the way in which one sentence is made to arise out of another, and to prepare the opening for a third: this is the great loom in which the textile process of the moving intellect reveals itself and prospers. Here the separate clauses of a period become architectural parts, aiding, relieving, supporting each other. (259; original emphasis)

Thus, carefully constructed paragraphs in which the sentences support each other facilitate the progression of thought that De Quincey sees as the heart of the rhetorical enterprise.

This attention to the mechanics of style merges smoothly with De Quincey's interest in the "organology" of style. In "Nexus in De Quincey's Theory of Language," Frederick Burwick argues that De Quincey perceives a strong connection between the "mechanology" and "organology" of style, as "the informing vitality of organic language is said to reside outside, or rather in between, its mechanical parts, in nexus" (263–64). Indeed, De Quincey's description of fanciful rhetorical activity consistently emphasizes the connection between the technical features of grammar and the underlying meaning of language and between style and content, which in his view facilitates the development of ideas that realize rhetoric's potential for creating intellectual depth. His brief discussion of the essayist John Foster concludes with the statement that "he could never have figured as a truly splendid rhetorician; for the imagery and ornamental parts of his Essays have evidently not grown up in the loom, and concurrently with the texture of the thoughts" ("Rhetoric" 110). This negative assessment contrasts with his praise for Edmund Burke, whose intellectually powerful arguments De Quincey perceives to be directly connected to style. According to De Quincey, Burke's rhetorical proficiency far exceeds that of Samuel Johnson, whose sentences contain ideas "fully preconceived," while in Burke, "every truth, be it what it may, every thesis of a sentence, *grows* in the very act of unfolding it. . . . [I]n Burke, whatever may have been the preconception, it receives a new determination or inflexion at every clause of the sentence" ("Rhetoric" 125n; original emphasis). Although Burke's critics perceive him as excessively layering his ideas with figurative images, De Quincey maintains that his rhetorical power comes from "thinking in and by his figures" ("Rhetoric" 115). De Quincey consistently emphasizes the systematic connection between style and thought, clearly admiring the writer's ability to use every aspect of style, including figures, sentence structure, and diction, to unify the development of the idea.

Unity in the midst of the complex exploration of thought is a central theme in De Quincey's treatment of style, as his repeated use of the "weaving" metaphor demonstrates. De Quincey's notion that rhetoric involves the free play of an idea is qualified by his insistence on the need for writers to reach beyond their internal consciousness in order to engage with themes that complement and expand their perspectives. The rhetor's discipline involves elaborating on an idea in a fanciful and recursive manner while weaving the entire work into a unified whole.

The interactions between mechanical and organic style exemplify the role of style in the dialogic process De Quincey conceives as central to rhetoric. He insists that style must foster the exploration of ideas, rather than serving as an empty vehicle for the outpouring of emotion. His criticism of the luxuriant style of Jean-Pierre Claris de Florian and Vicomte Chateaubriand ends with the complaint that there is "no flux and reflux of thought, half meditative, half capricious, but strains of feeling, genuine or not, supported at every step from the excitement of independent external objects" ("Rhetoric" 121). De Quincey also uses the negative examples of Robert Burton and John Milton to explain how extremes on one side or the other destroy the dialectical balance necessary for rhetoric. He explains that these writers exhibit "opposite defects" and then goes on to catalogue them at some length:

Burton is too quaint, fantastic, and disjointed; Milton too slow, solemn, and continuous. In the one we see the flutter of a parachute; in the other the stately and voluminous gyrations of an ascending balloon. Agile movement, and a certain degree of fancifulness, are indispensable to rhetoric. But Burton is not so much fanciful as capricious; his motion is not the motion of freedom, but of lawlessness; he does not dance, but caper. Milton, on the other hand, *polonaises* with a grand Castilian air,

in paces too sequacious and processional; even in his passages of merri-
ment, and when stung into a quicker motion by personal disdain for an
unworthy antagonist, his thoughts and his imagery still appear to move
to the music of the organ. ("Rhetoric" 102)

In contrast with Burton and Milton, De Quincey maintains that Jeremy
Taylor and Sir Thomas Browne perfectly exemplify this balanced use of
eloquence in their rhetorical writings. For this reason, he classifies them
as consummate rhetoricians, who "if not absolutely the foremost in the
accomplishments of art, were undoubtedly the richest, the most dazzling
and, with reference to their matter, the most captivating of all rhetoricians"
("Rhetoric" 104). In part, this "captivating" quality derives from the fact
that "in them only, are the two opposite forces of eloquent passion and
rhetorical fancy brought into an exquisite equilibrium" (104). According
to De Quincey, passion can serve rhetoric insofar as it facilitates an open
exploration of possibility, the strategic introduction of different tones and
perspectives that achieve rhetoric's dialogic potential.

Such an exploration requires a profuse array of ideas that can energize
discourse and careful control that sustains the development of key themes
throughout the exposition of those contrasting ideas. De Quincey describes
the prose of both Taylor and Browne as maintaining a harmonious pattern
that holds together the complex thoughts they present, as in a carefully
planned musical composition, "approaching, receding,—attracting, repelling,—blending, separating,—chasing and chased, as in a fugue,—and
again lost in a delightful interfusion, so as to create a middle species of
composition, more various and stimulating to the understanding than pure
eloquence, more gratifying to the affections than naked rhetoric" ("Rhetoric"
105). This approach can only be successful when the rhetorician possesses the
type of intellect that offers a rich array of interconnected ideas that come
to life organically during the development of the rhetorical composition:

> Where the understanding is not active and teeming, but possessed and
> filled by a few vast ideas (which was the case of Milton), there the funds
> of a varied rhetoric are wanting. On the other hand, where the under-
> standing is all alive with the subtlety of distinctions, and nourished (as
> Jeremy Taylor's was) by casuistical divinity, the variety and opulence
> of the rhetoric is apt to be oppressive. But this tendency, in the case of
> Taylor, was happily checked and balanced by the commanding passion,
> intensity, and solemnity of his exalted theme, which gave a final unity to
> the tumultuous motions of his intellect. ("Rhetoric" 108)

Veeder notes that Browne was generally appreciated by Romantics for prose that "focuses on self-awareness in relation to universal themes" ("Expressive Rhetoric" 103)—a quality that exemplifies De Quincey's interest in subjective investigation that has significance beyond the interests of the individual. In spite of what he describes as their "most opposite temperament" ("Rhetoric" 105), Taylor and Browne together exemplify De Quincey's precarious rhetorical ideal, which constructively manages the dialectical tensions between unity and diffusion, coolness and passion, careful control and limitless possibility.

The stylistic pattern of "approaching, receding,—attracting, repelling" reveals De Quincey's conception of the perfect style as embodying the dialogic process that lies at the heart of rhetoric's mission. De Quincey's style therefore anticipates Bakhtin's definition of style that "organically contains within itself indices that reach outside itself" ("Discourse" 284), as De Quincey points toward the capacity of language to manifest the strategic opposition of ideas, styles, and voices.

Style and History

In keeping with his usual methodology, De Quincey frames his discussion of both the mechanology and organology of style in a cultural and historical overview. He draws upon both ancient and modern history in supporting his contention that style is central to communication, even to the point of shaping and reflecting national identity. Because style is central to his conception of rhetoric, De Quincey's treatment of rhetoric's history often focuses on issues of language use. His proficiency with classical languages encourages attention to specific linguistic features that affect style and the presentation of ideas in Greek and Latin, which ultimately leads him to compare Greek rhetoric unfavorably with Roman: "The diffuseness and loose structure of Greek style unfit it for the closeness . . . of rhetoric. . . . In the literature of Rome it is that we find the true El Dorado of rhetoric, as we might expect from the sinewy compactness of the language" ("Rhetoric" 94–95). Thus, language and culture are intrinsically connected, with the two converging to affect the way in which thoughts develop and are expressed.

De Quincey's brief history of the evolution of style begins with the development of prose. He maintains that poetry naturally provided the vehicle for "public enunciations of truth" ("Style" 171) needed in early eras searching for divine inspiration. This view of poetry's role anticipates Bakhtin's view that the unity of poetry prohibits the full exploration of alternative possibilities ("Discourse" 285); according to De Quincey, prose came into being as society progressed and acquired an interest in earthly as well as heavenly reality. De Quincey states that "the arts of public speaking, and consequently of prose as opposed to metrical composition, have been the capital engine, the one great intellectual machine, of civil life" ("Style" 171). His identification of key figures who have contributed to the development of prose begins with Pherecydes ("Style" 173), whom he credits with the discovery of prose, and then moves to Herodotus, "the first respectable artist in prose" and Thucydides, "the first exhibition of stern philosophic prose" ("Style" 174). His survey, which he confines to "people of celebrity" ("Style" 180), next moves to the "House of Socrates," a group composed of Socrates, Plato, and Xenophon, whom he describes as "those who next attempted to popularize Greek prose" ("Style" 181). He prefaces his comments on this group with the interesting aside, "We acknowledge a sneaking hatred towards the whole household, founded chiefly on the intense feeling we entertain that all three were humbugs" ("Style" 181). De Quincey's explanation of his disdain for these "humbugs" is grounded in his view that unity is a central feature of stylistic excellence. His discussion of the style that characterizes the "House of Socrates" begins curiously with an aside about the use of aphorisms, which he describes as an accessible form for almost anyone, in contrast with the preferred prose style that develops ideas that are intricately connected. De Quincey again uses the metaphor of weaving in describing the value of style that brings disparate strains into a cohesive form: "The labour of composition begins when you have to put your separate threads of thought into a loom; to weave them into a continuous whole; to connect, to introduce them; to blow them out or expand them; to carry them to a close. All this evil is evaded by the aphoristic form" ("Style" 181). Although he acknowledges that the figures in question are not guilty of using aphorisms and that Socrates did not write at all, he apparently perceives the use of dialogue as similarly flawed in encouraging the presentation of ideas in isolation from each other. In De Quincey's view, this approach defines philosophy as the examination of "separate truths" ("Style" 184). Thus, De Quincey's account of the early history of prose articulates his conviction that style both demonstrates and fosters particular ideological and political commitments, as well as cultural tendencies.

Such assessments apply to modern societies, as well. In his survey of modern rhetorics of continental nations, De Quincey describes the Italian language as "too loitering for the agile motion . . . of rhetoric," adding that the national mind is "not reflective nor remarkably fanciful, the two qualities most indispensable to rhetoric" ("Rhetoric" 123). While he praises French preachers as the "only considerable body of modern rhetoricians out of our own language" ("Rhetoric" 124), he notes that their style also contains points of weakness, including "the defect of striking imagery; and, secondly, the slenderness of the thoughts" ("Rhetoric" 124). Because their thoughts tend to be pedestrian, they tend to be "unaffecting and trite unless varied and individualized by new infusions of thought and feeling" ("Rhetoric" 124–25). However, he expresses appreciation for the French attention to style, which exhibits a discipline lacking in English writers. Although he comments that sentence structure is inaccurately assumed to constitute the essence of style, he does take note of the French proficiency in this area ("Rhetoric" 126).

De Quincey generally upholds the historical superiority of British rhetoricians, but he laments the tendency to ignore stylistic matters. He notes Richard Whately's cursory treatment of style:

> In the age of our great rhetoricians it is remarkable that the English language had never been made an object of conscious attention. No man seems to have reflected that there was a wrong and a right in the choice of words, in the choice of phrases, in the mechanism of sentences, or even in the grammar. Men wrote eloquently, because they wrote feelingly; they wrote idiomatically, because they wrote naturally and without affectation; but, if a false or acephalous structure of sentence, if a barbarous idiom or an exotic word happened to present itself, no writer of the seventeenth century seems to have had any such scrupulous sense of the dignity belonging to his own language as should make it a duty to reject it or worth his while to remodel a line. . . . Hence, an anomaly not found perhaps in any literature but ours,—that the most eminent English writers do not write their mother tongue without continual violations of propriety. ("Rhetoric" 126–27)

De Quincey's emphasis on individual subjectivity in rhetorical practice does not completely deviate from eighteenth-century concerns with stylistic control and propriety. And, like the eighteenth-century theorists who preceded him, De Quincey perceives such disciplined language use as having both personal and social consequences.

Orality, Literacy, and Style

De Quincey shows a particular awareness of the challenge of acquiring the disciplined language use he considers to be the stylistic ideal in his discussion of style in nineteenth-century England. He suggests that the long history of successful oratory may in part be responsible for the British disinterest in written style. He notes that Greeks and Romans became attuned to "the magic of language" because their regular exposure to rhetoric "worked for purposes interesting to themselves as citizens, and sufficiently intelligible to command their willing attention" ("Style" 140). Although English people have had the same advantage, De Quincey maintains that they have not internalized the same sense, first of all because "the intertexture of style and substance" has often caused them to give credit to rhetorical content alone when they should have appreciated the unity of style and subject matter. The other cause relates to the shift from oral to written rhetoric. He explains that the styles of oral and written rhetoric are necessarily different. Oratory requires repetition, for "where each sentence perishes as it is born, both the speaker and the hearer become aware of a mutual interest in a much looser style, and a perpetual dispensation from the severities of abstract discussion" ("Style" 140). Repetition and amplification, therefore, are necessary in oratory, as the speaker provides the audience ample opportunity to absorb the ideas that are being presented, "all which, being the proper technical discipline for dealing with such cases, ought no longer to be viewed as a licentious mode of style, but as the just style in respect of those licentious circumstances" ("Style" 140). For people accustomed to oratory to appreciate the distinct features of written style therefore requires a shift in sensibility, as *the modes of style appropriate to popular eloquence being essentially different from those of written composition,* any possible experience on the hustings, or in the senate, would *pro tanto* tend rather to disqualify the mind for appreciating the more chaste and more elaborate qualities of style fitted for books" ("Style" 141; original emphasis). At the same time, he recognizes that oratory does not easily translate into written texts. He comments that published sermons cannot capture the vitality of those that have been delivered verbally, hence, "[n]o pulpit oratory of a rhetorical cast for upwards of a century has been able to support itself when stripped of the aids of voice and action" ("Rhetoric" 110). Thus, the English appreciation for oral political eloquence has actually worked against the general awareness of the characteristics of style, particularly written style, that De Quincey hopes to cultivate.

At the same time, De Quincey sees the proliferation of print as an opportunity for writers and readers to acquire appreciation for style. He identifies the lack of opportunities for publicity in Greece as diminishing what otherwise might have been a strong interest in style, given his theory that "subjective branches of study favour the cultivation of style" ("Style" 229). De Quincey's subsequent discussion of the impact of a lack of publicity for writers constitutes a section of the essay that Hudson highlights as significant in providing "clues to a whole branch of rhetorical study, a branch dealing with the technique of publicity in its relation to the rhetorical and literary expression of a given period" (211). De Quincey explains that because Greek writers had no outlet for consistently publishing their works, they had no reason to devote energy to refining work that was unlikely to be seen by those outside their immediate circle of acquaintance ("Style" 232). After a lengthy excursus on the chief obstacle standing in the way of publicity for Greek writers, which he identifies as the lack of paper rather than the inability to print, De Quincey concludes that the limitations on writing ensured that Greek public discourse centered upon the theater and the agora, which limited interest in other genres and ultimately inhibited the development of a comprehensive theory of style in Greece.

De Quincey notes that in England, on the other hand, the explosion of opportunities for publication has made it possible for writers to imagine that they will have readers, whether this is actually the case or not ("Style" 240). This consciousness should encourage writers to be attentive to style, to be aware of "the vast importance of compression," to unite the "culture of an unwordy diction . . . with the culture of clear thinking" ("Style" 235). Print, therefore, entails particular responsibilities with respect to style but also offers unique opportunities that have not been available to cultures that lack the publicity available through print. In part, this comes about through the permanence of print, which enables people to examine prose style at greater leisure. In contrast with oral speech, "[i]t is the advantage of a book that you can return to the past page if anything in the present depends upon it" (139). While in oral discourse, "[t]ime must be given for the intellect to eddy about a truth, and to appropriate its bearings" (140), the permanence of print allows writers and readers to develop an approach to language use that involves a different type of discipline. It is De Quincey's hope that this opportunity can be carried forth in a way that will ultimately promote clearer thinking, the beginning of a cycle that could ultimately contribute to the development of better writing—and more profound intellectual engagement.

Style and Nineteenth-Century Culture

In spite of the opportunities for stylistic development afforded by publicity, De Quincey sees his own culture as losing ground in the corresponding areas of effective writing and clear thinking. Although print can be a potentially positive force in the development of stylistic consciousness, he sees British books and newspapers, the type of printed material most readily available to the public, as sadly lacking in the stylistic qualities that people should cultivate. Like many of his contemporaries, De Quincey adopts the ironic position of attacking the very press that publishes his own work, including his diatribes against the poor writing that he blames for society's decline. Christopher Kent notes that during this period, "[t]he power of the press, real or imagined, fascinated Victorian writers" (5). This fascination undoubtedly reflected the recognition that "[i]n the nineteenth century the newspaper became an increasingly central element in the representation of everyday reality, in creating the code of realism that affected the way readers conceived and perceived the world" (Kent 4). De Quincey's assumptions about the power of newspapers to shape the public's consciousness prompt his charges that the writing styles most frequently found in the press provide poor models for language use, which he conceives as weakening both the oral and written discourse found in the surrounding society.

One of De Quincey's chief complaints about the writing styles most frequently encountered in print relates to pretentious diction. He charges that most writers are essentially careless about language use but substitute true attention to style with imprecise phrasing that does not enhance the communication of ideas. This phenomenon leads to what De Quincey identifies as style that experiences "the pressure of two extremes: of coarseness, of carelessness, of imperfect art, on the one hand; of spurious refinement and fantastic ambition on the other" ("Style" 144). The example of both extremes interferes with what De Quincey describes as the preferable stylistic mode, a more natural, colloquial, conversational manner of expression. Although he understands that oral and written speech inevitably differ, De Quincey insists that written language should nevertheless maintain the clarity and spontaneity of oral speech. In contrast, he maintains that books have promoted "diction too remote from the style of spoken idiom" and asks, "But why is it that in our day literature has taken so determinate a swing towards this professional language of books as to justify some fears that the other extreme of the free colloquial idiom will perish as a living dialect?" ("Style" 148). In responding to this question, De Quincey focuses on newspapers, which constitute the reading material most widely distributed to the public.

De Quincey's discussion of newspapers includes some recognition of the practical factors that have contributed to what he sees as their inferior style. He acknowledges that the focus of newspapers is inevitably on public business, the factual orientation that he consistently identifies as an obstacle to full attention to style, and that the need to publish newspapers quickly supports careless sentence structures, particularly giving rise to the "plethoric form of period, this monster model of sentence" ("Style" 150). De Quincey's assessment of the negative impact of the stylistic flaws newspapers exhibit is harsh, which is not surprising, given his conviction that the manner of expression is inextricably linked to the message communicated. The ability of newspapers to impart knowledge is therefore seriously jeopardized by their inferior prose style. After pointing to newspapers as the exemplars of the poor style he has criticized, De Quincey adds, "The Evil of this, as regards the quality of knowledge communicated, knows no remedy" (149). This statement clearly demonstrates De Quincey's conviction that because style and substance are joined, an obscure style inevitably damages the strength of the ideas that are shared.

But, for De Quincey, the public's inability to receive clear information from newspapers is by no means the only problem. He describes the social changes that take place as language evolves, with specific attention to the shift from a primary emphasis on orality to literacy, as he depicts public language use as seriously influenced by journalistic style. According to De Quincey's account, the nature of this influence is largely a negative one, as he notes that people traditionally learned to communicate naturally and then came to study the writing found in books, but in the current cultural environment, "the whole artificial dialect of books has come into play as the dialect of ordinary life" ("Style" 149). Because the public has such ready access to newspapers, De Quincey perceives the types of stylistic flaws found in newspapers, including convoluted sentence structures, as achieving prominence in speech patterns across all sectors of society. He describes at some length the challenges people face in trying to express their innermost thoughts using diction and sentence structures that they have absorbed from written texts. Undoubtedly, some of De Quincey's attention to this issue relates to his awareness of the changing demographic found among newspaper readers and his assumption that people who read inferior prose without an adequate educational background will be particularly vulnerable to its bad influence; as Richard D. Altick points out, "It was principally from among skilled workers, small shopkeepers, clerks, and the better grade of domestic servants that the new mass audience for printed matter was recruited during the first half of the century" (83). De Quincey alludes to this fact in expressing the opinion that the pedantic speech patterns found in newspapers have become common among people of every social station, a trend most people do not even notice. De Quincey identifies two specific stylistic flaws that one typically encounters in British society: "Separately from this change for the worse in the drooping idiomatic freshness of our diction, which is a change that has been going on for a century, the other characteristic defect of this age lies in the tumid and tumultuary structure of our sentences" (153). He perceives the two problems to be related, as people's affinity for Latin derivations found in books has encouraged them to develop both diction and sentence structures that correspond to Latin rather than English. These habits, according to De Quincey, have resulted in a popular style that "has laboured with two faults that might have been thought incompatible: it has been artificial, by artifices peculiarly adapted to the powers of the Latin language, and yet at the very same time careless and disordinate" (153–54).

The combination of artificial and careless language use is perhaps inevitably seen as a negative cultural influence to someone with De Quincey's keen sense of the important connection between language and intellectual development. Indeed, he argues, "[p]edantry, though it were unconscious pedantry, once steadily diffused through a nation as to the very moulds of its thinking, and the general tendencies of its expression, could not but stiffen the natural graces of composition, and weave fetters about the free movement of human thought" ("Style" 152). Moreover, people are unwilling to read carefully when they encounter prose so dense and unnecessarily complicated that it is difficult to follow. De Quincey insists that people develop strategies for "shorthand" reading in order to avoid their encounters with periodic style, which ultimately leads to the "incorrigible habit of desultory reading" (162). This leads not only to poor reading practices but also results in a "reaction upon a man's faculties," the diminution of "his judging and reasoning powers" (162). De Quincey, therefore, portrays an unfortunate cycle that has blighted his society's intellectual development, as the growth of print has altered both the public's reading methods and communication styles. This phenomenon has, in turn, diminished the intellectual strength and creative mental energy that must be preserved in order to maintain society's vitality.

De Quincey does offer some hope that the spontaneity of natural discourse can be preserved. He notes that the French have avoided the worst features of English style, in spite of the fact that they are just as inclined to be inattentive to the fine points of language use. De Quincey argues that the French are able to maintain a type of clear communication that has been lost to the British because they are "a nation of talkers" ("Style" 155). Due to their cultural circumstances, the French have persevered in writing sentence structures that reflect conversational principles: "brief, terse, simple; shaped to avoid misunderstanding and to meet the impatience of those who are waiting for their turn" (156).

While it might not be possible to convert England to become "a nation of talkers," De Quincey interestingly identifies women as those who might offer hope for British language. He notes that in Britain, as in Rome, the purity of idiomatic language use can be found primarily among women and children. He acknowledges that there are women who are published authors but does not include them in his positive assessment; instead, he sees the best communication style as preserved by "well-educated women not professionally given to literature" ("Style" 142). He perceives women as less prone to the high-flown prose that leads to a detachment between style and sense, arguing that they are more inclined to speak with truth and simplicity. De Quincey attributes this strength both to biological difference and social circumstance, noting that "there is always something in the situation of women which secures a fidelity to the idiom" (144). Part of this situation is the result of the distinct sensibility that women exhibit toward their surroundings; their strong feelings give rise to the types of urgent situations that demand an authentic response. Thus, De Quincey's view that "real feeling shuts out all temptation to the affectation of false feeling" (145) leads him to point toward the correspondence of women as models for good style, specifically, "that class who combine more of intelligence, cultivation, and of thoughtfulness, than any other in Europe—the class of unmarried women above twenty-five—an increasing class; women who, from mere dignity of character, have renounced all prospects of conjugal and parental life, rather than descend into habits unsuitable to their birth" (145). While women may preserve standards of good style in idiomatic use, De Quincey notes that certain types of writing, including "the higher forms of history or philosophy" (146), should exhibit a different style; for this type of writing, in Britain, as in ancient Rome, "purity of diction" is preserved by women and "people of rank" (146). Thus, De Quincey's hope that effective language use can be maintained in certain areas of industrial society is bounded by both class and gender.

De Quincey's writing about style and gender constitutes what Marie Secor describes as "some of his strangest, most whimsical statements," but she adds, "Quirky as such a statement appears at first glance, a second glance discloses its assumptions and suggests a sense in which it can be taken seriously" (79). This interpretation focuses on the consistency in De Quincey's view that style "not corrupted by imperfectly assimilated bookishness" can be found "in informal, unpretentious writing (therefore letters), the most spontaneous of which are most likely, in his view, to be produced by unliterary but not unlettered women" (79). Angela Leighton also focuses on what she describes as "a quite distinct gender politics of style" in this passage, an examination that falls within her larger investigation of De Quincey's complicated relationship with women. She observes that De Quincey "found women the objects of natural identification and affection" and notes that his insistence that unmarried women are the repositories of good style means that "sense of style . . . is in direct proportion to their lack of conjugal and parental control" (166–67). Leighton, therefore, points out that De Quincey's connection between unmarried women and unaffected style draws him into an acknowledgment of "the power complexes of the lives of actual women" (166). Thus, although De Quincey's characterization of women's style can be seen as essentializing women's experiences and language use, he can also be seen as considering ways in which women might pursue opportunities for the leisurely play with language that he advocated by working within and against the cultural restrictions that surrounded them. While De Quincey's conclusions about language and gender do not readily connect with contemporary thinking, his assumption that positive consequences are available to those isolated from full participation in industrial society is at least consistent with a worldview that sees in industrial society an undesirable repression of human creativity.

Style in De Quincey's Dialogic Rhetoric

De Quincey's sense that styles of communication have generally declined reinforces his broader argument about rhetoric's enervation due to the strictly practical orientation of industrial society. His effort to provide not a manual of style but "a psychology of the scene of its production" (Camlot 81) leads De Quincey to engage critically with the conditions that limit the development of the stylistic complexity that contributes to the exploration of the opposing perspectives that lie at the heart of complex thought. His argument concerning the detrimental effects of modern society's practical priorities reflects an anxiety about public standards that De Quincey shared with other nineteenth-century writers. Raymond Williams describes how the relationship between writers and readers changes during this period: "Writers had, of course, often expressed, before this time, a feeling of dissatisfaction with the 'public,' but in the early nineteenth century this feeling became acute and general" (33), an attitude that Williams identifies as particularly evident in the writings of Wordsworth.

De Quincey sees the possibility for a positive change in the public's appreciation of style through the cultivation of a "culture of style" ("Style"

226) attentive to the capacity of language to energize thought through the juxtaposition of opposing intellectual motions. Style is, therefore, an integral component of De Quincey's vision of a rhetoric that offers the disciplined exploration of complex ideas and multiple possibilities. Hudson identifies the connection between style and invention as creating a degree of unity in De Quincey's theory: "De Quincey teaches that the rhetorical process, the process of *presenting an idea attractively*, whether as a display of power, in play, in poetic exuberance, or for a persuasive purpose, involves an inner and an outer activity. The inner activity we may call rhetorical invention; the outer, rhetorical style" (205; original emphasis). Talley also describes De Quincey's placement of style at the center of rhetoric's persuasive activity, stating that for De Quincey, "[s]tyle not only provides pleasure, but is an observable extension of the individual's ethical, and probably his logical, proof" (253). Thus, De Quincey generates a notion of style that lies at the heart of the rhetorical enterprise, as it fosters creative exploration but draws the rhetor into dialogue with other people and other points of view.

The relationship between style and invention, therefore, assigns to style a central role in De Quincey's dialogic rhetoric. De Quincey advocates the development of style that is simultaneously organic and mechanic, internally focused and externally constrained, fostering a subjective exploration of thought that "reaches outside itself" (Bakhtin, "Discourse" 289) in order to achieve new intellectual discoveries. He envisions the outcome of this dialogic enterprise with language as the creation of what Camlot refers to as "a culture of style, which will in turn allow for the more widespread occurrence of true publication—of sympathy between writers and readers" (86).

De Quincey uses his "science of style" to present new challenges to a society that he perceived as immersed in the mediocre prose of the popular press. His exposition of the relationship among rhetoric, style, and culture reveals his sense of the social significance that underlies the challenge he offers. In De Quincey's view, style has historically been recognized as achieving its purpose both through careful attention to the guidelines that foster effective style and through practice that demonstrates the unity of matter and manner. A key feature of De Quincey's work involves drawing together the strands of *rhetorica docens* and *rhetorica utens* ("Style" 216), theory and practice, in his writing about rhetoric. In this and the preceding chapter, I argue that De Quincey's essays advance a rhetorical theory in spite of their untraditional form; the following chapter examines how De Quincey's application of his dialogic rhetorical theory in his own writing demonstrates the conversion of theory into practice.

CHAPTER 5

De Quincey's Writing: Dialogic Rhetoric in Action

De Quincey's presentation of his ideas about rhetoric defies expectations for cohesion and consistency that traditionally surround the genre of the rhetorical treatise. Embedded in De Quincey's notion of rhetoric is the presumption that systematic accounts of how rhetoric should function jeopardize the subjective dialogue that defines the rhetorical enterprise. To devise a rhetorical treatise geared toward prescribing rhetoric's role in public life would, therefore, undermine De Quincey's insistence that rhetoric should provide creative individuals with opportunities to explore ideas freely and to allow that exploratory process to infuse society with the intellectual energy that he believed to be endangered by the imposed values of science and industry. Style is an important component in this creative process, as the rhetor develops and demonstrates intellectual vitality through the strategic use of language.

Scholars who have attempted to understand De Quincey through comparing his work to the expositions on rhetoric found in traditional treatises are understandably frustrated in their efforts to convert De Quincey's wide-ranging discussion into a more systematic and accessible form. A more productive avenue for understanding De Quincey's thinking about rhetoric is to attempt to appreciate the very features that make it so unique. Lawrence D. Needham argues that many criticisms of De Quincey's "Rhetoric" come from "critics who have refused to read 'Rhetoric' on its own terms, as a bravura performance of verbal display" (49). It is the premise of this book that the project of appreciating De Quincey's rhetorical theory entails first tracking key themes that emerge through the course of De Quincey's writings on rhetoric and language, which I have undertaken to do in chapters 3 and 4. The next step in understanding De Quincey's view of rhetoric involves observing how he enacts his vision of rhetoric through his own writing. The goal of this chapter is to delineate how De Quincey illustrates and illuminates his theory through his own rhetorical practice.

De Quincey's Rhetorical Practice

In *Thomas De Quincey, Literary Critic: His Method and Achievement*, John E. Jordan refers to De Quincey's despair over the death of rhetoric but goes on to note that De Quincey was "apparently oblivious of how exquisitely much of his own writing fits his definition of rhetoric" (218). Frederick W. Haberman offers a different interpretation, as he goes so far as to argue that much of what can be found in De Quincey's rhetoric is intended to describe only his own practices: "De Quincey formulated not just one theory of rhetoric, but two: a theory of rhetoric or of literature as intellectual play for Thomas de Quincey, and a theory of rhetoric as persuasion for the rest of the world. . . . As a practicing author, rhetoric as delight was a branch of literature which De Quincey reserved for himself. Being a stunt pilot, in short, he needed a specially designed plane" (199–200). While I would argue that De Quincey did not intend to reserve his theory for himself, I agree with Haberman's claim that De Quincey saw his work as intricately connected to the principles he upheld and with his conclusion that "De Quincey was his own best practitioner; his work illustrates in every degree of excellence his own theory" (201).

However, if it is indeed the case that much of De Quincey's way of defining rhetoric can be found in his own writing, defining the precise principles that guide De Quincey's rhetorical performance is nevertheless a challenging task. De Quincey's impressive corpus covers a wide range of subjects, genres, and purposes. Early twentieth-century critic Sherwin Cody describes De Quincey's work as "extremely miscellaneous in character" (116), a characterization supported by the fact that De Quincey wrote over two hundred essays dealing with topics ranging from autobiography to political economy. Although it is not always possible to state with certainty what any writer's purposes are, the goals of De Quincey's writing appear to vary and to include entertainment, self-expression, cultural criticism, argument, and, without a doubt, financial remuneration. Given the volume and diversity of De Quincey's work, it is impossible to make broad generalizations about characteristic rhetorical strategies that appear across the varied time periods, genres, and moods in which De Quincey wrote.

However, it is possible to see in De Quincey's approach a direct enactment of his view that rhetoric involves a writer's dialogic engagement with a range of ideas and multiple possibilities. His writings consistently illustrate Don Bialostosky's description of the focus of dialogics, the pursuit of "comprehensive responsiveness and responsibility to the consequential person-ideas of a time, culture, community, or discipline—that is, for the fullest articulation of someone's ideas with the actual and possible ideas of others" ("Dialogics as an Art" 789). Across his literary corpus, De Quincey's rhetorical strategy involves an intricately woven pattern that juxtaposes personal reflection, cultural and historical background, encounters with other people, and investigation of varying approaches to a subject, a technique that aptly illustrates key premises of his view of rhetoric.

De Quincey's capacity for considering alternative perspectives begins with what Jason Camlot describes as the division that defines his attitude as a writer: "De Quincey embodies a rare combination of reverence (for Wordsworthian romanticism) and cynicism (resulting from his experience as a professional writer)" (76). In part, this divided consciousness emerges as a function of De Quincey's life and the conditions in which he wrote. E. Michael Thron argues that De Quincey

> was standing in a different place from that of the poets. . . . [H]e saw himself as the object and the subject, as the observed and the observer, in one—as the "idol" and the "priest." It follows that if he converted his daily struggle into his writing, with or without opium, the fragmentation of the way he had to work would shape his prose. This transparency between the demands of the periodical press and his prose becomes as much a subject for De Quincey as anything else he experienced. (8)

Needham points out that De Quincey's consciousness of the material factors surrounding his craft played an important role in his conception of his work: "Far from being divorced from actuality, De Quincey's rhetoric of display constitutes his response to the very real demands of publication and the exigencies of the marketplace" (50). Camlot echoes this view, noting that De Quincey faced "the predicament of identity for one who had hoped to arrive at coherence and unity but was forced into fragments by the generic demands of the periodicals market" (75). Julian North identifies audience awareness as a key factor that shapes De Quincey's writing, as she suggests the need "to recognize De Quincey's statements in relation to the reading public, in his magazine journalism, as themselves constructions of and communications with the audience for whom he is writing at that moment" ("Wooing the Reader" 99). Thus, De Quincey's consciousness of a complex array of external factors was woven into the content of his writing and his representation of his own subjectivity.

Many of De Quincey's writings reflect his deliberate participation in what he describes as a central task of rhetoricians, "eddying about their own thoughts" ("Rhetoric" 121); at the same time, those writings consistently expand the boundaries of subjective experience outward in order to avoid what he described as "the dust and rubbish of individuality" ("Rhetoric" 119). Edward Sackville-West argues that De Quincey's "object in writing was not to give his readers isolated sensations, but to make them aware of implications in life of which they might be unconscious, but which it had been his privilege, through a highly special medium of pain and sorrow, to experience and analyse" (332). While the didactic motives that Sackville-West appears to attribute to De Quincey are debatable, De Quincey's effort to connect individual interests to broader concerns not only reflects the exigencies imposed upon him by the economic conditions under which he wrote but also can be seen as an explicit principle in his rhetorical theory that he consistently pursues in his writings.

De Quincey's exploration of the inextricable links between the individual's personal experience and the surrounding culture can be seen as a fundamental premise that crosses much of his work. In his first autobiographical essay, De Quincey begins by introducing his father's particular situation, moves immediately to present the perspective of a contemporary individual in similar circumstances, shifts to a discussion of the situation of a prominent individual from the past, and then briefly connects the entire conversation to history before returning in the following paragraph to the original subject of his father:

> My father was a plain and unpretending man, who began life with what is considered in England (or *was* considered) a small fortune, viz., six thousand pounds. I once heard a young banker in Liverpool, with the general assent of those who heard him, fix upon that identical sum of six thousand pounds as exemplifying, for the standard of English life, the absolute *ideal* of a dangerous inheritance; just too little, as he said, to promise comfort or *real* independence, and yet large enough to operate as a temptation to indolence. Six thousand pounds, therefore, he considered in the light of a snare to a young man, and almost as a malicious bequest. On the other hand, Ludlow, the regicide, who, as the son of an English baronet, and as ex-commander-in-chief of the Parliament cavalry, etc., knew well what belonged to elegant and luxurious life, records it as his opinion of an Englishman who had sheltered him from state bloodhounds, that in possessing an annual revenue of £100, he enjoyed all the solid comforts of this life,—neither himself rapacious of his neighbour's goods, nor rich enough in his own person to offer a mark to the rapacity

of others. This was in 1660, when the expenses of living in England were not so widely removed, *oequatis oequandis*, from the common average of this day; both scales being far below that of the long war-period which followed the French Revolution.

What in one man, however, is wise moderation, may happen in another, differently circumstanced, to be positive injustice, or sordid inaptitude to aspire. At, or about his 26th year, my father married. ("Parentage" 1:17–18; original emphasis)

Thus, in slightly over one paragraph, De Quincey reveals to the reader that his father's economic situation will be interpreted through a lens the writer provides, which immediately includes what De Quincey has overheard people say about finances, his knowledge of the lives of other prominent individuals, history, and language, and his awareness of his mother's point of view.

De Quincey's pattern of drawing attention to the interconnections among personal experiences, his subjective interpretations of those experiences, and his knowledge of the outer world appears in a wide array of his writing. His autobiographical works consistently press outward into history and culture, as is evident when he interrupts his narrative account of his own travels to devote two chapters to the first and second Irish rebellions. At the same time, his explorations of history and literature inevitably circulate within and are shaped by his own consciousness and reflect his belief in the significant connections that exist between people and between individuals and their cultural surroundings. Sackville-West states that De Quincey's approach to history involved "a processional method of approach to historical events and characters which suited his own very special vision of the world" (257), a subjective perspective to history writing that De Quincey embraced without apology and made explicit to the reader in various ways. His typical approach to his literary biographies mirrors his autobiographical essays, as he intricately juxtaposes information about the life of the writer, the writer's significance, and the historical period surrounding that individual's life.

De Quincey's literary essays provide further examples of his unique ability to bring together cultural insights, personal reflections, and historical background. His acclaimed essay "The English Mail-Coach," published in *Blackwood's* in 1849, exemplifies the interdependence of historical events, personal actions, cultural developments, and the individual's inward life expressed in dreams. De Quincey begins the account with a whimsical statement about the invention of the mail coach, which he then connects with his personal experience of riding the mail coach as an Oxford student:

Some twenty or more years before I matriculated at Oxford, Mr. Palmer, at that time M.P. for Bath, had accomplished two things, very hard to do on our little planet, the Earth, however cheap they may be held by eccentric people in comets: he had invented mail-coaches, and he had married the daughter of a duke. He was, therefore, just twice as great a man as Galileo, who did certainly invent (or, which is the same thing, discover) the satellites of Jupiter, those very next things extant to mail-coaches in the two capital pretensions of speed and keeping time, but, on the other hand, who did *not* marry the daughter of a duke.

These mail-coaches, as organized by Mr. Palmer, are entitled to a circumstantial notice from myself, having had so large a share in developing the anarchies of my subsequent dreams. (13:270–71)

The remainder of the essay continues the pattern of weaving together themes that include the cultural significance of the mail coach, the events and people surrounding De Quincey's experiences with that form of transportation, the dreams engendered by De Quincey's experiences, and the role of the mail coach in spreading information about the Napoleonic Wars throughout the countryside.

De Quincey's complicated connection between individual and social is mediated through the intimacy of the relationship he establishes with the reader. In "A Brief Appraisal of the Greek Literature," De Quincey describes Edmund Burke's skill as residing in his ability to "enrich what is meager, elevate what is humble, intellectualise what is purely technical, delocalise what is local, generalise what is personal," all made possible by the "silent understanding between the orator and his audience" (334)—an understanding he seeks to cultivate through a prose style that guides the reader through the elaborate meanderings of his thought. While Burke's relationship with the audience is created through oratory, De Quincey creates a "silent understanding" that is uniquely possible through the medium of print, which he, in turn, both embraces and critiques. John C. Whale describes the intricate balance De Quincey maintains in connecting with the periodical reader: "Through a series of appeals to the reader De Quincey not only promotes a mediatory device in keeping with the confessional aspect of his work but also confirms the magazine identity of his writings. . . . Although the form of writing may well be described as familiar, it is a familiarity set up to challenge certain notions of publicity" (37). In spite of the fact that De Quincey undoubtedly feels what Lee Erickson describes as the tendency of nineteenth-century writers to "feel alienated both from their own work and also from the common reader" (188) due to changing publishing technologies, he strategically establishes a connection to the reader through exploiting the tension between intensely private writing and a reading public that is much larger than had been possible only a few decades before. De Quincey's interactions with notions of privacy and publicity, along with his juxtaposition of his own divergent identities, accessible to the reader through his public confessional text, further heightens the irony that underlies his demonstration of dialogic rhetoric.

The union of style and substance that De Quincey advocates in "Style" and admires in Burke, whom he praises for "thinking in and by his figures" ("Rhetoric" 115), can also be seen as a strategy that De Quincey frequently employs. While many of his writings seem simply to reflect De Quincey's conviction that "agile movement, and a certain degree of fancifulness, are indispensable to rhetoric" ("Rhetoric" 102), he also aspires to the "exquisite equilibrium" he appreciates in Jeremy Taylor and Sir Thomas Browne ("Rhetoric" 104). He consistently maintains a tight structure that allows for strategic digressions that at times appear to stray from the subject at hand but ultimately circle back to the central point. Although Margaret Oliphant's 1877 essay on De Quincey titled "The Opium-Eater" is generally critical of De Quincey, Oliphant does acknowledge De Quincey's prose as possessing a unique spaciousness in the author's development of the topic: "No tripping from subject to subject, no light abandonment of one theme for another, but unconscious, beautiful growth, expansion, efflorescence outward and upward, until the slight text has blossomed out into a system of doctrine" ("Rhetoric" 741). Oliphant's description captures the "eddying" motion that De Quincey advocates for rhetorical practice, along with the fanciful and luxuriant engagement with language that he describes as a feature of rhetoric's contribution to a vital intellectual life. At times, De Quincey offers the reader explicit guidance through the windings of his thought. He begins the chapter of his autobiographical reflections titled "Premature Manhood" with a summary of the preceding chapters that concludes with the acknowledgment that the reader may find the threads that connect De Quincey's reflections elusive at times:

> Somewhat arbitrary episodes, therefore, are these two last chapters; yet still endurable as occurring in a work confessedly rambling, and whose very duty lies in the pleasant paths of vagrancy. Pretending only to amuse my reader, or pretending chiefly to—*that*, however much I may have sought, or *shall* seek, to interest him occasionally through his profounder

affections, I enjoy a privilege of neglecting harsher logic, and connecting the separate sections of these sketches, not by ropes and cables, but by threads of aerial gossamer. (1:316; original emphasis)

In his following paragraph, De Quincey insists, "I am now returning into the main current of my narrative," but he defers returning directly to the narrative of his early life by starting the next paragraph with the question, "But when, by what test, by what indication, does manhood commence?" While his reflections on this topic cover territory that may appear to be abstract in nature and far removed from the anticipated account of De Quincey's early adventures, De Quincey's philosophical reflections on this topic provide him with the necessary foundation for illuminating his insights into the significance of the personal events he later recounts.

The pattern of weaving together a complex array of ideas lies at the heart of De Quincey's rhetorical practice across his literary corpus. In his analysis of De Quincey's writing strategies in book reviews and literary essays, Hoyt H. Hudson takes note of De Quincey's habit of surrounding simple ideas, "the logical or factual skeleton," with extensive variations, a reflection of De Quincey's assumption that "if the reader is to be interested, the thought must be exhibited from more angles and must be related to other interesting ideas" (206). A striking example of the intricacy with which De Quincey fantastically elaborates and then connects the fanciful images that develop his thought is in "The English Mail-Coach." De Quincey's initial discussion of his infatuation with the coachman's granddaughter Fanny includes the statement that the coachman resembled a crocodile in his "monstrous inaptitude for turning round" (13:286). He later builds on this conceit in a playful passage that returns to the crocodile, describes that creature's timeless character in exaggerated and comical terms, and then juxtaposes that quality with the change that otherwise pervades the world De Quincey depicts in this essay focused on his personal encounters with time and the intrepid motion of the mail coach:

The Fannies of our island—though this I say with reluctance—are not visibly improving; and the Bath Road is notoriously superannuated. Crocodiles, you will say, are stationary. Mr. Waterton tells me that the crocodile does *not* change,—that a cayman, in fact, or an alligator, is just as good for riding upon as he was in the time of the Pharaohs. *That* may be; but the reason is that the crocodile does not live fast—he is a slow coach. I believe it is generally understood among naturalists that the crocodile is a blockhead. It is my own impression that the Pharaohs were also blockheads. Now, as the Pharaohs and the crocodile domineered over Egyptian society, this accounts for the singular mistake that prevailed through innumerable generations on the Nile. The crocodile made the ridiculous blunder of supposing man to be meant chiefly for his own eating. Man, taking a different view of the subject, naturally met that mistake by another: he viewed the crocodile as a thing sometimes to worship, but always to run away from. And this continued till Mr. Waterton changed the relations between animals. (13:288; original emphasis)

Following a footnote that describes Mr. Waterton as a naturalist from a previous generation who made a public display of riding a crocodile, De Quincey goes on to insist that this feat reveals that "the final cause of man is that he may improve the health of the crocodile by riding him a-foxhunting before breakfast," adding that this proves that "any crocodile who has been regularly hunted through the season . . . will take a six-barred gate now as well as ever he would have done in the infancy of the pyramids" (13:288). De Quincey then makes a transition from this remarkable passage to further reflections on the mail coach, Fanny, and her grandfather, which lead him back to the essay's theme of the passage of time: "If, therefore, the crocodile does *not* change, all things else undeniably *do*: even the shadow of the pyramids grows less. And often the restoration in vision of Fanny and the Bath road makes me too pathetically sensible of that truth" (13:289; original emphasis). De Quincey's sensibility leads him to reflect on a number of images connected with Fanny, the mail coach, and the reptilian driver, which in turn connects with the dreams that form another major theme in the essay: "[O]nce again the roses call up the sweet countenance of Fanny; and she, being the granddaughter of a crocodile, awakens a dreadful host of semi-legendary animals—griffins, dragons, basilisks, sphinxes—till at length the whole vision of fighting images crowds into one towering armorial shield, a vast emblazonry of human charities and human loveliness that have perished" (13:289). Thus, De Quincey demonstrates the expansive thought that can be pursued through language that fosters playful and adventurous connections but at the same time maintains the balance and structure necessary to the development of new ideas.

De Quincey's effort to consider imaginative links between disparate ideas also connects to his rhetorical technique of "giving an impulse to one side" ("Rhetoric" 91), a tactic of investigation that ultimately entails an ironic recognition of the possibilities and limitations of his own position. In "Grazing the Brink: De Quincey's Ironies," Jordan argues that De Quincey's use of irony deserves greater notice: "[T]he world of the Opium-Eater was richly ironic. He lived on the edge of chaos which he was continually creating and re-creating, which horrified and intrigued him, at which he marveled, shuddered, and mocked, from which he generated considerable energy, and in which he found occasional islands of calm" (199). In his analysis of the tensions embedded in De Quincey's use of the East, Daniel Sanjiv Roberts charges that much De Quincey criticism "only reads De Quincey on his own terms of unity and coherence: a critical seduction that we should resist" (37). Roberts adds that "a better recognition of developmental and sometimes contradictory strains in his writings would be more helpful in achieving a correct understanding of his work" (37). While Roberts points to ways in which these internal conflicts are likely unintentional on De Quincey's part, Barry Milligan states that "throughout 'The Pleasures of Opium,' De Quincey does in a more focused, even exaggerated way what he does throughout the *Confessions* in particular and his whole oeuvre in general: he wryly notes, critiques, and celebrates the tendency of supposed dichotomies to collapse upon themselves" (46).

This ironic opposition permeates a wide range of De Quincey's writings. In the case of "On Murder Considered as One of the Fine Arts," an 1827 *Blackwood's* essay, De Quincey establishes strategic conflict through creating two authorial voices, neither of which can be taken entirely seriously. The body of the essay is a lecture delivered to an organization called the Society of Connoisseurs in Murder, which is introduced by "a man morbidly virtuous," who insists that he publishes the lecture in order to bring the organization's evil intentions to light: "For my intense virtue will not put up with such things in a Christian land" (13:9–10). The lecture that follows provides a direct counterpoint to the introduction in offering a compelling discussion of the artful practice of murder: "People begin to see that something more goes to the composition of a fine murder than two blockheads to kill and be killed, a knife, a purse, and a dark lane. Design, gentlemen, grouping, light and shade, poetry, sentiment, are now deemed indispensable to attempts of this nature" (13:12). De Quincey's lecturer subsequently issues an aside "to certain prigs, who affect to speak of our society as if it were in some degree immoral in tendency" (13:12). While the lecturer acknowledges that "murder is an improper line of conduct, highly improper" (13:12), he goes on to complicate this assessment by drawing the reader's attention to alternative ways of interpreting even this act: "Everything in this world has two handles. Murder, for instance, may be laid hold of by its moral handle (as it generally is in the pulpit and at the Old Bailey), and *that*, I confess, is its weak side; or it may also be treated *aesthetically*, as the Germans call it—that is, in relation to good taste" (13:12; original emphasis).

Even in De Quincey's more argumentative pieces, such as his spirited defense of Tory politics in "A Tory's Account of Toryism, Whiggism, and Radicalism," (*Tait's Edinburgh Magazine*, 1835–36), he acknowledges the complex intersections that exist among apparently opposing positions. This recognition leads him to admit that the three parties have similar imperfections that are not always acknowledged: "Even in private disputes, where one party is violent, personal, overbearing, rapid, and visibly on the fret to interrupt at every moment, the wisest and the coolest feel it difficult to resist the contagion of the case. My party, therefore, if it does not already, very soon *will* adopt the tone of its antagonists" ("Tory's" 9:316; original emphasis). De Quincey's celebration of collapsing dichotomies, alongside the images of energy and calm, reflection and fancy, and suspension and motion that are emphasized in his depiction of the ideal in rhetorical style, establishes patterns of opposition that enact the dialogic rhetoric he advocates in principle.

De Quincey's exploration of the conflicts that surround complex ideas at the same time reveals an attention to style that fulfills the central goals of maintaining the clarity and connections that promote "intelligibility" while managing "to regenerate the normal *power* and impressiveness of a subject which has become dormant to the sensibilities" ("Language" 260; original emphasis). De Quincey consciously demonstrates the interaction between organic and mechanical style that he highlights in his essay on style. Sackville-West describes De Quincey's writing in the essay on Scottish philosopher Sir William Hamilton as balancing stylistic freedom and control, as he developed a "free associational kind of writing that was to have no parallel until James Joyce and Virginia Woolf systematized it into a method of deliberate art" (244). Cody acknowledges the criticism of the "Dream-Fugue" that constitutes part 3 of "The English Mail Coach" but adds that "we should lose the point and meaning of it if we failed to note how every lyrical image in this part of the composition corresponds to a prose fact in the first and second parts. The logical relationship is perfect, and is elaborated with the utmost thought and care" (117).

This complex pattern of connections and stylistic techniques can be seen through a careful examination of De Quincey's "Rhetoric" and "Style," as well as *Confessions of an English Opium-Eater*. In "Rhetoric" and "Style," he illustrates the "eddying" of ideas derived from his unique knowledge of varied disciplines, time periods, and sources, all woven together in what ultimately becomes a whole argument, albeit one that at times follows an unpredictable and somewhat erratic course of development. De Quincey's exploration of his own opium use in *Confessions* repeatedly pushes against the boundaries that define the circumstances of his life, the unique cultural values that surround his historical moment, and the reader's beliefs about drug addiction. These texts, therefore, demonstrate varying strategies comprising De Quincey's approach to rhetoric, revealing how he harnesses what appear to be chaotic principles in order to develop essays and autobiographical writings that combine rhetorical fancy and passionate eloquence.

Struggling with the "Burden of the Incommunicable"

In addition to its other personal revelations, the *Confessions* contains a detailed and explicit examination of the frustrations De Quincey has experienced in communicating with his mother. His account of his visit home following his escape from the Manchester Grammar School reveals,

> My mother was predisposed to think ill of all causes that required many words: I, predisposed to subtleties of all sort and degrees, had naturally become acquainted with cases that could not unrobe their apparellings down to that degree of simplicity. If in this world there is one misery having no relief, it is the pressure on the heart from the *Incommunicable*. And, if another Sphinx should arise to propose another enigma to man—saying, What burden is that which only is insupportable by human fortitude? I should answer at once—*It is the burden of the Incommunicable*. (315; original emphasis)

In this short passage, De Quincey articulates the deep-seated fear that he will find it impossible to communicate his perspective to a world that, like his mother, is inclined "to think ill of all causes that required many words"—and in the process explains why it is necessary that he do so. This passage articulates tensions that are not only present in De Quincey's relationship with his mother but are also inherent in his textual production, as he highlights what seems to be an inevitable gap between the individual's internal sensibility and the perceptions of the external world, even as his subtle and verbose text asserts his determination to overcome that gap.

De Quincey's ironic position is represented in other questions he invites concerning his motives in producing the text. In the preface to the original 1822 edition, De Quincey explains that he has created his account in hopes that "it will prove not merely an interesting record, but, in a considerable degree, useful and instructive" (*Confessions* 3:209). He further maintains that only this desire to be of service to the reader has enabled him to overcome his reticence in writing about his experience: "*[T]hat* must be my apology for breaking through that delicate and honourable reserve which, for the most part, restrains us from the public exposure of our own errors and infirmities" (3:209; original emphasis). Yet, De Quincey immediately undercuts the establishment of his rhetorical ethos, as the narrative of his experiences proves not to be strictly the cautionary moral tale his preface appears to promise. His ostensible focus on "the moral of my narrative" (3:213) is at odds with his acknowledgment that "my way of writing is rather to think aloud, and follow my own humours, than much to consider who is listening to me" (3:413–14). Thus, De Quincey asserts the value of subjective inquiry that lies at the heart of rhetoric and at the same time illustrates the intellectual flexibility available through that process.

De Quincey continues to demonstrate his commitment to a rhetorical position that moves between opposing alternatives as he begins the narrative portion of the *Confessions*. Following his response to those who have questioned the cause of his initial decision to take opium, he shifts to an argumentative stance that counters the more apologetic tone he used in the preface. While he states clearly that he turned to opium "on a sudden, overmastering impulse derived from bodily anguish" (3:224), he then adds, "Meantime, without blame it might have been otherwise. If in early days I had fully understood the subtle powers lodged in this mighty drug (when judiciously regulated) . . . I should have inaugurated my opium career in the character of one seeking *extra* power and enjoyment, rather than of one shrinking from *extra* torment. And why not? If *that* argued any fault, is it not a fault that most of us commit every day with regard to alcohol?" (3:224; original emphasis). Thus, the *Confessions* overturns any expectation the reader might have had that De Quincey's desire to be instructive will lead him to adopt a penitent position from the outset.

Charles J. Rzepka argues that *Confessions* must be viewed as a text that reflects in complicated ways the material circumstances that surrounded De Quincey's writing, a factor that adds to the layers of ironic opposition that surround the text. Rzepka claims that embedded in the text is the financial need that drove De Quincey to write, a need that De Quincey chooses not to acknowledge. His construction of the book therefore involves "repeatedly representing itself as a gift rather than as a commodity, and its author as a bestower of gifts rather than a writer for hire" (17). While Rzepka notes that it should not necessarily be expected that De Quincey, or any author, would discuss the financial aspects of literary production, he finds it "significant that the writer should take pains to raise and exorcise this expectation repeatedly throughout the work. Why, after all, *should* the opium-eater confess . . . ? . . . Promising a 'useful and instructive' tale warning us of the woe that attends taking the drug, De Quincey spends about as much of his narrative on the delights of opium's artificial paradise as on the monsters hiding in it" (17).

Needham, too, highlights the interplay of conflict as a key element of the rhetorical strategy De Quincey uses in setting up the *Confessions*:

> The opium-eater initiates a narrative wherein he portrays himself as a "victim of circumstances—familial, constitutional, social." The language he employs to justify his revisionary account . . . throws a rhetorical cast over his "Preliminary Confessions" and suggests, in particular, that he is applying to his situation the colors of rhetoric. . . . His efforts to place his actions in a positive light are reminiscent of the "sophistry" of declamatory exercises in which speakers often extricated their character from indefensible or impossible situations by elaborating extraordinary motivations or extenuating circumstances. (55)

Robert Morrison points toward other political conflicts that are deeply embedded in the text of the *Confessions*: "Drugs in De Quincey's *Confessions of an English Opium-Eater* are simultaneously poison and cure, public and private, paradise and prison, natural and artificial. Critics for the most part have read the *Confessions* as endorsing De Quincey's deep-seated conservatism. But his political outlook in the text is almost as unstable as his opium intake" ("'Earthquake'" 63). De Quincey occupies the complex and at times contradictory positions in the *Confessions* that he identifies as a necessary element in rhetoric's capacity to engage with multiple possibilities. Morrison argues that even the character of the author is affected by these patterns of opposition, as De Quincey "is both hero and anti-hero. . . . De Quincey's racial and aristocratic prejudices co-exist with his intense sympathy for the exiled and the abused" ("'Earthquake'" 65). Thus, both De Quincey's personal identity and his political perspective are defined by the patterns of conflict that the text highlights.

These conflicts provide evidence of De Quincey's commitment to rhetorical indeterminacy, which continues to be evident throughout his development of the *Confessions*. His decision to explore both poles of his experience with opium, highlighted in the headings "The Pleasures of Opium" (3:379) and "The Pains of Opium" (3:412), suggests that even drug use may fall under the category of "cases where there is a *pro* and a *con*, with the chance of right and wrong, true and false, distributed in varying proportions between them" ("Rhetoric" 91). De Quincey masterfully draws the reader's attention at one moment toward one possible interpretation of his situation, while at another moment he offers another. His transition from "The Pleasures" to "The Pains" provides an example of the eloquence that marks particular passages of the *Confessions*: "But now farewell, a long farewell, to happiness, winter or summer! Farewell to smiles and laughter! Farewell to peace of mind, to tranquil dreams, and to the blessed consolations of sleep! For more than three years and a-half I am summoned away from these. Here opens upon me an Iliad of woes" (3:411). Yet, De Quincey's subsequent account of the "pains" he has suffered through opium is continually qualified by points that contrast with those detrimental effects. Parts of his narrative certainly offer a poignant account of the difficulties his excessive use of opium caused for him: "In thus describing and illustrating my intellectual torpor, I use terms that apply, more or less, to every part of the years during which I was under the Circean spells of opium" (3:433). At the same time, he also credits his initiation into opium use with the arrest of the hereditary pulmonary disease that had led to his father's early death (3:424–25). He admits that opium has generated vivid dreams based in events from his past life and is, therefore, the "cause of shadowy terrors that settled and brooded over my whole waking life" (3:434); however, his insistence upon the ease with which he was able to control his opium use when he exerted himself remains part of the record he provides. In fact, he draws attention to and heightens the effect of the oppositions in his narrative when, after a digression concerning the effect of opium use on an application for life insurance, De Quincey adds,

> Here I pause. The reader will infer, from what I have now said, that all passages, written at an earlier period under cloudy and uncorrected views of the evil agencies presumable in opium, stand retracted; although, shrinking from the labour of altering an error diffused so widely under my own early misconceptions of the truth, I have suffered them to remain as they were. My general views upon the powers and natural tendencies of opium were all supported and strengthened by this fortunate advantage of a professional correspondence. (3:429)

At this point, it is difficult to be sure which point De Quincey really would be interested in retracting, but it is also clear that he has strategically circumvented his own authorial agency.

In the process, De Quincey creates a narrative in which the properties of opium hold remarkable similarities to the dialogic qualities of rhetoric he has outlined. Like rhetoric, opium contains the inventive potential for acquiring multiple perspectives: "For opium *is* mysterious; mysterious to the extent, at times, of apparent self-contradiction; and *so* mysterious that my own long experience in its use—sometimes even in its abuse—did but mislead me into conclusions ever more and more remote from what I now suppose to be the truth" (3:414; original emphasis). De Quincey's explanation that the deception of opium draws him away not from the truth but from what he *now supposes* to be the truth leaves open the possibility that opium offers a different truth—a suggestion De Quincey underscores at various points in his narrative. Like Gorgias, who argues that "[t]he effect of speech upon the condition of the soul is comparable to the power of drugs over the nature of bodies" (46), De Quincey suggests a relationship between language and drugs. Both are "mysterious" and capable of "self-contradiction," and in those qualities lie the pleasures both language and opium hold: "O just, subtle, and all-conquering opium! That, to the hearts of rich and poor alike, for the wounds that will never heal, and for the pangs of grief that 'tempt the spirit to rebel,' bringest an assuaging balm;—eloquent opium! That with thy potent rhetoric stealest away the purposes of wrath" (3:393). In this passage, De Quincey strategically moves from the fanciful rhetoric that dominates much of the *Confessions* to invoke the passionate eloquence that he is capable of commanding, in the process highlighting the ways in which opium, like rhetoric, contains a vital power that is difficult to harness. In describing opium as "eloquent" and in possession of a "potent rhetoric," De Quincey weaves together his pleasurable rhetorical struggle with the "burden of the incommunicable" with all of the contradictory mysteries he has found in opium.

Rhetorical Practice as Theory

In his *Confessions*, De Quincey deploys his use of fanciful discourse and eloquence in order to explore freely the range of experiences he has had with opium. In the process, he demonstrates his awareness of the possibilities and limitations of language to overcome "the burden of the incommunicable." While his effusive and elaborate discursive investigation of his autobiography and opium use provides him with the means to approximate the subtlety and ambiguity of the world he has experienced, the mysteries of language, like those of opium, are elusive.

De Quincey's awareness of the difficulty of harnessing language is evident in his rhetorical practice and in his essay on rhetoric, which provides a complex exploration of rhetoric's potential without resorting to the prescription the audience might look for. Chapter 2 has already discussed the theory of rhetoric De Quincey articulates in "Rhetoric." This chapter returns to analyze that essay in order to argue that it not only contains much of the content of De Quincey's rhetorical theory but also exemplifies the rhetorical practices that his theory describes.

Although De Quincey's essay is framed as a review of Richard Whately's *Elements of Rhetoric*, he begins not with a reference to Whately but with the notion that rhetoric has historically existed in a state of flux: "No art cultivated by man has suffered more in the revolutions of taste and opinion than the art of Rhetoric" ("Rhetoric" 81). The brief historical survey of rhetoric's varied incarnations that follows this statement provides De Quincey with the opportunity to establish an ironic position in keeping with the pattern he creates in the *Confessions*: "Such is the popular idea of Rhetoric; which wants both unity and precision" (82). While De Quincey's goal certainly involves dismantling "the popular idea of Rhetoric," he will not do so through creating the straightforward "unity and precision" that the reader might expect. He instead develops a subtle organic unity through the complex interplay of ideas that he perceives to lie at the heart of rhetorical practice—a type of unity available to the reader patient enough to track the elaborate wanderings that De Quincey will take through history, various contemporary cultures, and the inner workings of his own mind.

De Quincey's suggestion that "the formal teachers of Rhetoric" will not aid the reader seems straightforward in light of his explanation of the shortcomings of both George Campbell and Whately. However, De Quincey's subsequent endorsement of Aristotle again points toward the possibility that De Quincey has been ironic in his rejection of "formal teachers," given that Aristotle's work is generally viewed as the epitome of formalized rhetoric. Yet, De Quincey complicates the picture further by revising Aristotle to suit his own purposes. Thus, the dynamic interplay between De Quincey's internal perspective and the external world is established in his deliberate appropriation of the rhetorical tradition, represented by Aristotle, to suit his own purposes; just as he creates an intimate relationship with the reader of the *Confessions*, he describes his interpretation of Aristotle in a manner that conveys an almost personal relationship with history, as he justifies his reading based on "a suggestion derived from him" (83). He immediately acknowledges that others may advance interpretations that differ from his, but he appears confident that his perspective holds the potential to create dramatic reverberations in the wider world: "Our explanation involves a very remarkable detection, which will tax many thousands of books with error in a particular point supposed to be as well established as the hills. We question, indeed, whether any fulminating powder, descending upon the schools of Oxford, would cause more consternation than the explosion of that novelty which we are going to discharge" (85). At the same time, the very force of this dramatic claim encourages in the reader some doubt about whether De Quincey seriously believes that his theories of Aristotle hold as much consequence as he appears to claim for them.

De Quincey's presentation of a private reading of Aristotle with public implications resides in the very practice his essay advocates, "giving an impulse to one side" ("Rhetoric" 91). In setting out to offer "colourable support" (86) for his position, De Quincey demonstrates the fanciful work with language that he defines as rhetoric's primary task. After identifying probability as the heart of Aristotle's rhetoric, De Quincey juxtaposes a definite assertion with a question that raises doubts about the credibility of that very claim, as he acknowledges that his interpretation may depart from Aristotle's understanding of his own theory: "That this was the real governing law of Aristotle's procedure it was not possible to doubt: but was it consciously known to himself?" (86). This question propels him forward into a lengthy investigation of the enthymeme, which includes a survey of varied commentaries that ultimately support his earlier interpretation of rhetoric's role in dealing with contingent matters (90–91).

From this point of focus, De Quincey's discussion ranges across variations on the themes he has established, as he explores the distinctions between rhetoric and eloquence ("Rhetoric" 92), surveys the varied conceptions of rhetoric found in the histories of ancient Greece and Rome (93–96), and seamlessly returns to a consideration of rhetoric's place in modern Europe. The remainder of his essay weaves in and out among his assertions concerning the dynamic relationship between rhetoric and its surrounding culture and his critical exploration of that premise as manifested in the work of particular British writers and orators. This section is followed by a discussion of the rhetoric of continental Europe, which enables De Quincey to elaborate further on his themes of rhetoric, culture, and political life. Only in the final pages of his essay does De Quincey return to Whately, ostensibly the subject of his essay, who, instead, seems to have become something of an afterthought. De Quincey's reference to the strength of French sentence structure appears to remind him that he is discussing style, which he acknowledges to be "the subject of the third part of the work before us" (126). From that point, he winds in and out of references to specific features of Whately's treatment of style, ending with the somewhat startling conclusion, "[W]e suppose it hardly necessary to add that Dr. Whately's is incomparably the best book of its class since Campbell's *Philosophy of Rhetoric*" (133). While this statement appears rather suddenly at the end of a lengthy discussion that had not led systematically toward the claim, De Quincey might have seen this conclusion as one that emerges gradually and subtly through the windings of his thoughts on rhetoric. His expectation that the reader could fill in the gaps that he had not explicitly addressed illustrates his view that the suppression of one premise of the enthymeme reflects the typical patterns of human thought, since "Nature sufficiently prompts all men to that sort of ellipsis" (87). In this way, De Quincey allows the reader to work through the connections that have led him to conclude his remarkable odyssey with a return to the two works with which he began. While his initial assessment of them offers an explication of points in which the two depart from his own interpretation, De Quincey's final observation demonstrates his ability not only to maintain a unifying thread in the midst of what at times might have appeared to be rhetorical chaos but also to use his elaborate exposition of ideas in order to weave his way toward a deeper appreciation for concepts than would be available through a more cursory examination.

Although a number of scholars have noted significant differences between De Quincey's essays on rhetoric and style, including a twelve-year gap in their publication dates, the two demonstrate not only common patterns in his thinking about rhetoric and culture but also similarities in his approach to rhetorical practice. As in the case of "Rhetoric," De Quincey begins "Style" with a sentence that focuses the reader's attention on time, diverging ideas, and multiple possibilities: "Amongst the never-ending arguments for thankfulness in the privilege of a British birth—arguments more solemn even than numerous, and telling more when weighed than when counted, *pondere quam numero*—three aspects there are of our national character which trouble the uniformity of our feelings" (134). A whimsical exploration of these problematic aspects provides the framework for De Quincey's leisurely journey toward his essay's central point, the English neglect of style, "which tends in all things to set the matter above the manner" (137).

As in his essay on rhetoric, De Quincey interrupts the circular motion of his ideas to provide the reader with a clear statement of his position that anchors the remainder of the essay: "This general tendency operates in many ways: but our own immediate purpose is concerned with it only so far as it operates upon Style. In no country upon earth, were it possible to carry such a maxim into practical effect, is it a more determinate tendency of the national mind to value the *matter* of a book not only as paramount to the *manner*, but even as distinct from it, and as capable of a separate insulation" ("Style" 137; original emphasis). However, this clear statement of purpose is followed by a lengthy paragraph, extending through the following page, that elaborates on this idea in ways that gradually move outward into an examination of the relationship between language and culture. The course of the essay continues to evolve in cycles that draw the reader through varied cultural dynamics and historical periods, always circling back to De Quincey's central focus on British style.

Throughout the essay, De Quincey alternates sections that move the argument forward with further elaborations of notions that invite the reader to explore the internal workings of his mind. De Quincey follows the statement that British authors "are distinguished by the most absolute carelessness" in style ("Style" 141) with copious variations on that theme, including investigation of historical parallels, a discussion of careless practices of assigning names, and the general "use of the existing language" (144). This point again propels De Quincey toward a circular exploration of cultural diversity, history, and gender, culminating in the observation that "we are satisfied . . . that they, the educated women of Great Britain . . . are the true and best depositaries of the old mother idiom" (146). This point and the discussion that evolves from it ultimately facilitate De Quincey's clearly stated diagnosis of the problem: "The whole artificial dialect of books has come into play as the dialect of ordinary life" (149).

The following pages provide support for this position, not through the linear progression of the argument but through an exploration of the manifestation of this artificiality in British language use, with treatments of foreign languages offered as points of contrast, and the consequence of this artificiality on the reading habits of the British public. This discussion again moves De Quincey forward, as his thinking on this subject enables him to articulate the claim that "it is by the effects reflected upon his judging and reasoning powers, that loose habits of reading tell eventually" ("Style" 162). De Quincey finally moves toward the conclusion of the essay's first section by synthesizing the general themes of culture, conversation, and writing in his theory of the "organology" and "mechanology" of style (163–64), which provide a backdrop for the remainder of the essay.

The second section of the essay shifts to an expansive investigation of history, with particular attention to the stylistic foundations provided by the Greeks. While this portion of the essay maintains its connection to the general theme, De Quincey feels obliged to begin the third section with an address to the reader that acknowledges the lengthy digression that he has allowed himself: "Reader, you are beginning to suspect us. 'How long do we purpose to detain people?'" ("Style" 189). This expression of sympathy with the reader does not, however, lead him to return quickly to the subject of British style but instead prompts him to detail the course he will take with his next digression, as he explains that he plans to "detain you a little longer on the Grecian Prose Literature; and we shall pursue that Literature within the gates of Latium" (190). Thus, De Quincey's consciousness of the reader's potential impatience with his digression leads him not to repent and return to the course the reader might be expecting but simply to assure the reader that he is fully in control of the essay's progress, whether or not that appears to be the case.

Following this assurance, De Quincey devotes the remainder of part 3 to a continued investigation of ancient theories and practices of style, which continues with his discussion of *rhetorica docens* and *rhetorica utens* in part 4 ("Style" 216). De Quincey's discussion of the distinct features of style exemplified in the Greek conception of rhetoric "as a practicing art, *rhetorica utens*" (217) brings him to a contemporary comparison, as he asserts that "style in our modern sense, as a theory of composition, as an art of constructing sentences and weaving them into coherent wholes, was not effectually cultivated among the Greeks" (218). From this point, he returns to immerse himself in a discussion of Greek literature, after which he moves into a brief discussion of Medieval rhetoric before pausing to "retrace the course of our speculation, lest the reader should suppose us to be wandering" (225). Thus, De Quincey again acknowledges the suspicion that he might not be efficiently advancing his initial argument concerning British style but does so in a way that actually enables him to linger longer on the periphery of that discussion.

As if recognizing the limits of the reader's ability to follow the development of his thought, however, De Quincey does eventually offer a direct summary of the purpose that has guided his exposition: "We have made this digression by way of seeking, in a well-known case of public life, an illustration of the difference between a subjective and an objective exercise of the mind" ("Style" 229). This sentence helps to bring into focus a new line of inquiry for De Quincey, which includes the relationships among subjective and objective study and theoretical and practical approaches to style, which, in turn, leads to an investigation of the bearing publicity has upon style. Although much of De Quincey's discussion appears to focus on ancient Greece, it ultimately leads him to infer intriguing connections between a culture in which a lack of publicity leads to inattentiveness toward style and one in which excessive publicity has the same effect.

The structure and development of both "Rhetoric" and "Style" rely upon the expanding and contracting motions of De Quincey's thought—a rhetorical strategy that differs markedly from that advocated in the treatises that constitute much of the rhetorical canon. De Quincey's construction of these texts serves as both a cause and effect of his exclusion from that canon, as he provides a discussion of rhetoric that can be seen as providing neither the practical public rhetoric exemplified in the tradition of *rhetorica utens* nor the accessible instruction associated with *rhetorica docens*. De Quincey's essays do not contribute a unified theory that readily corresponds to the systems that have generally dominated rhetorical history, and for that very reason they demonstrate the rhetorical practice that De Quincey offers as the basis for the intellectual revitalization of his society. Although De Quincey's prose undoubtedly illustrates the "eddying about" of ideas that he advocates, it also demonstrates his awareness that "[t]he labour of composition begins when you have to put your separate threads of thought into a loom; to weave them into a continuous whole; to connect, to introduce them; to blow them out or expand them; to carry them to a close" ("Style" 181). De Quincey's expectation that the reader will labor with him in discovering the connections that underlie his prose arises from his determination to enact his own rhetorical theory, as he challenges the reader to a new level of intellectual engagement through the complexity of his text.

De Quincey's Conversational Practice

Chapter 3 argues that one of the distinguishing features of De Quincey's expansive notion of rhetoric is his inclusion of conversation in his treatment of socially significant language practices. His insistence that British style could be strengthened through infusing the stilted prose people absorb from the press with the spirited style of conversation is reflected in his own writing style, which Sackville-West describes as informed by the principles of conversation: "Like Lewis Carroll, he had all the shyness of the scholar. He therefore takes refuge in the anonymity of essay-writing, where he may indulge his brilliant conversational power with the utmost freedom. De Quincey's essays are therefore delightfully conversational, though they are the product of the solitary imagination" (115). De Quincey's conversational style helps to establish the intimate relationship with the reader that creates a bridge between his internal thought processes and his audience. It also sustains the blurring of public and private that is a characteristic feature of De Quincey's rhetorical theory.

In addition to adopting a conversational style in much of his writing, De Quincey cultivated conversation as an art form that enabled him to acquire a rhetorical identity that otherwise would not have been available to him. Many of the characteristics of this form are consistent with other qualities he values in rhetoric. In both the essay on conversation and the *Confessions*, De Quincey refers to his own conversation as a model for the theory he advocates. His assessment of his own rhetorical success in this regard was apparently not exaggerated. In his description of De Quincey's trip to Edinburgh with Jack Wilson in 1814, Sackville-West eloquently describes De Quincey's conversational powers: "[H]e would slide gently—almost imperceptibly—into the conversation, with a kind of whisper—low-toned, weird and musical. And at once the talk would be lifted . . . into an iridescent, kaleidoscopic half-world lit by a livid gleam of the talker's own making and peopled with the half-recognized creatures of his extraordinary genius" (141). An acquaintance of De Quincey, Robert Pearse Gillies, describes the attributes of De Quincey's conversation in ways that correspond to the characteristics De Quincey advocates in written rhetoric: "Whatever the subject might be, every one of his sentences (or of his chapters, I might say) was woven into the most perfect logical texture, and uttered in a tone of sustained melody" (qtd. in Sackville-West 141). Even Carlyle, who was famous for his frank, critical judgment of his contemporaries, referred to De Quincey in an 1833 letter to philosopher John Stuart Mill as "one of the prettiest talkers I ever heard" (qtd. in Sackville-West 229). Another striking testimony to the power of De Quincey's conversation can be found in a passage from the 1877 letter from Robert Carruthers to A. H. Japp, which describes De Quincey's remarkable conversational powers: "I had heard Rogers and other conversationalists, but was overpowered by De Quincey's flow of melodious talk" (item 88). In another letter to Japp, Carruthers reiterates the mesmerizing effect of De Quincey's conversation: "I listened with intense pleasure and surprise to his musical voice and eloquent periods for at least six hours!" (25 March 1877, item 89).

While one might assume that De Quincey's fame in this area might be the result of a dominant conversational style, Sackville-West insists that this was not the case:

[T]his was the ultimate marvel which distinguished De Quincey's conversation from, and thus far raised it above, that of Coleridge and Carlyle—his talk was never a monologue. . . . However fantastic the castle he built, he would always pause in the building to invite advice and suggestions, before proceeding to a further stage; then, when he had made others talk, he would gather up what they had laid out and, like a conjuror with a folded piece of paper, twist them in a moment into the oddest and most unexpected shapes. But those who listened never felt that they were a mere audience. (142)

De Quincey's commitment to drawing other people into his discourse, weaving their ideas into the fanciful intellectual play of his own conversation, demonstrates his application of the principles of dialogic rhetoric in his approach to conversation—and points toward his conviction that conversation is a significant social act that promotes sympathy and social responsibility.

De Quincey as Rhetorician

De Quincey's innovative and idiosyncratic approach to rhetoric offers an intriguing alternative strain that builds on and departs from earlier articulations of rhetoric's social function. His contribution is supported in large measure by a personality that represents the expansive intellect, unique perspective, and internal tensions that lie at the heart of his rhetorical theory. The fame of De Quincey's style has at least in some measure rivaled his reputation as an "opium-eater"; in her survey of the critical reception of De Quincey's work, North presents Richard Garnett's 1884 edition of the 1821 text of the *Confessions* as an example of the increased interest in De Quincey's style in the 1880s and 1890s: "The quality of the life lived by the author and the moral value of the narrative for his readers are simply ignored. What is interesting to Garnett is the beauty of the style in which the *Confessions* are written. . . . For Garnett, then, the form of De Quincey's autobiography is not merely more remarkable than its substance, it is its substance" (50). This effusive style reflects De Quincey's conviction that "every truth . . . *grows* in the act of unfolding it" ("Rhetoric" 125; original emphasis). This unfolding process involves the use of the "reflective" and "fanciful," which De Quincey identifies as "the two qualities most indispensable to rhetoric" ("Rhetoric" 123). Balancing rhetoric's work of reflection and fancy can be seen as one way of ensuring the "new infusions of thought and feeling" that are crucial to the ongoing motion De Quincey advocates for rhetoric.

Of course, De Quincey, like every writer, has his detractors. Some critics suggest that his strategic digressions are at times not adequately managed and that De Quincey's prose is difficult to follow, a problem perhaps exacerbated by De Quincey's drug use and by the rapid pace of his production. Hudson perceives De Quincey as lacking in the concerted attention to audience that would ensure his success as a rhetorician: "He thought that one was only a *pure* rhetorician when he gave his fancy free rein to wander where it would. But we can hardly grant that one is a good rhetorician, or even a mediocre one, when he forgets his audience and his theme and his purpose, prime factors, all of them in the rhetorical equation. Perhaps this one defect was all that barred De Quincey from being supreme in persuasive art" (210; original emphasis).

While this assessment aptly recognizes a key area in which De Quincey's rhetoric departs from classical models of the communication triangle, Hudson fails to consider the possibility that De Quincey establishes an alternative relationship with the audience that holds the potential for a different type of rhetorical supremacy. Certainly, De Quincey eschews the goal of guiding the audience to a clear judgment about a specific claim. Like Mikhail M. Bakhtin's Socrates, whom James Zappen describes as "restoring to the rhetorical tradition the multiplicity of voices that Bakhtin believes are always there" (14), De Quincey enacts a dialogic rhetoric that offers an intriguing counter to a discipline that has often been seen as dedicated to gaining the audience's adherence to a predetermined conclusion. In strategically replacing the strict bonds of logic with "threads of aerial gossamer" ("Premature Manhood" 1:316), De Quincey provides an intriguing point of resistance to the audience-based standard that had guided rhetoric's development for centuries—and serves as an early instance of the shift in nineteenth-century British prose writing from the unified ethos assumed throughout much of the rhetorical tradition to the "quickened and multiplied consciousness" (Buckley 182) that Walter Pater seeks at the end of the century. De Quincey by no means "forgets" audience, theme, and purpose but instead weaves a rich tapestry of ideas and images aimed at inspiring new insights and a deeper appreciation for language.

CHAPTER 6

De Quincey's Place in Rhetorical Histories

Thomas De Quincey's rhetorical theory and practice offers a modern alternative to classical theories that define rhetoric in terms of an interaction among speaker, text, and audience directed toward addressing specific civic questions. De Quincey's writings about rhetoric, language, and style draw upon his interpretation of classical and modern rhetorical theories, criticism of historical and contemporary writers and speakers, and examinations of the complex relationship between language and culture. While these resources provide a degree of coherence between De Quincey's thought and that of earlier strains in the western rhetorical tradition, De Quincey's idiosyncratic perspectives on history and his unique interpretation of key texts regularly disrupts established assumptions surrounding the rhetorical theories he cites. This disruption is by no means an accident on De Quincey's part. His historical and educational interests inspire his belief in the importance of building his work on established intellectual foundations; at the same time, his aim is to argue for the individual's power to reconfigure those foundations through intensive intellectual exploration of alternative possibilities. According to De Quincey, that exploration takes place in the realm of rhetoric, which has a tradition that provides useful boundaries for inquiry and a nature that encourages the ongoing reimagining of those boundaries.

De Quincey's innovative perspective responds to and participates in major changes that take place in British rhetoric's public and private functions during the nineteenth century. This book began with the premise that Richard Whately's *Elements of Rhetoric* should not be seen as the conclusion of nineteenth-century British rhetoric. De Quincey's rhetoric occupies a pivotal position between more traditional rhetorics, as represented by Whately, and the new vocabularies for rhetoric that evolve in the nineteenth century. De Quincey's thought, therefore, offers valuable insight into strains in British rhetorical history that have previously been overlooked.

In crafting a discussion of rhetoric and style that engages with the concerns of industrial society, De Quincey establishes a connection between his work and that of theorists and writers in the latter decades of the nineteenth century. In the conclusion of his chapter on De Quincey, Jason Camlot writes, "De Quincey's awareness of the effects of the growing publishing industry upon the British reading audience, and his conception of style not only as an aesthetic category but as a matter of psychological and social significance, mark the parameters of discussions and debates about style in writing as a manifestation of the modern individual for the rest of the century" (87). Marie Secor notes that De Quincey's rejection of the "hierarchical view of style" (79) constitutes a turning point in which "[t]he classical notion of distinct levels of style becomes irrelevant . . . when the boundaries between levels are blurred by the exigencies of mass publication and the ubiquity of jargon" (80). She further points out that De Quincey's broadened perspective leads him to identify style as "more than one science: it can look at words on the page and explore their interrelationships; or it can examine relationships between the elements of the rhetorical triangle, the speaker, the discourse, and the transaction between them" (80). Secor also notes that De Quincey's view that the aesthetic features of style appeal both to the intellect and the emotions in reactivating the power of the subject builds on the work of early theorists such as George Campbell and Whately and anticipates Herbert Spencer's *Philosophy of Style*, while his famous claim that style serves as the incarnation of thought anticipates the thought of Walter Pater late in the century. Thus, Secor recognizes De Quincey's theory of style as a central moment in the transition from eighteenth-century rhetorical theory to later theories in rhetoric and criticism.

De Quincey also anticipates the nineteenth-century trend toward an emphasis on literary criticism as an art form in itself, a move that facilitates the transition from traditional approaches to rhetoric to the growing interest in aestheticism that characterizes the latter half of the nineteenth century. John E. Jordan states that De Quincey considered "the *subject* of criticism his métier, more than its practice" (introduction 34; original emphasis), a view that foreshadows prominent cultural critic Matthew Arnold's later notion of the critic as a social prophet. Julian North cites author Richard LeGalliene's 1898 argument "for De Quincey as a precursor of the late-century aesthetes," noting that LeGalliene "sees De Quincey as having anticipated such prose-artists as Walter Pater in emancipating their medium 'from the drudgery of knowledge'" (51). Camlot also notes the influence of De Quincey's notion that "[s]cholarship is not associated with knowledge gathered from books, but rather with the ability to organize and project the inner mind" (85). De Quincey's interest in the unconscious nature of "literature of knowledge" foreshadows the theoretical approaches of Scottish journalist and critic E. S. Dallas, as well as Pater and Oscar Wilde. His description of the vitality available through the "eddying about" of thoughts that both intersect with and resist external concerns also anticipates Pater's discussion of critical insights shaped by cultural conditions, but developing under "the comparatively inexplicable force of a personality, resistant to, while it is molded by, them" (111).

De Quincey's insistence upon the dialogic exploration of possibility as a counter to scientific certainty also anticipates an ongoing trend as the century moves forward to employ paradox as an intellectual challenge to industrial society. Ruth Robbins describes the project of Decadent aesthetics as breaking through the rigid social categories that many intellectuals had come to see as placing limitations on the expression of individual identity, which led fin de siècle writers such as Vernon Lee to adopt rhetorical positions that explicitly embraced contradiction (141). Jonathan Freedman echoes this view, stating that "the defining quality of British aestheticism—the only way these various and distinctive writers and artists may be seen to share any characteristic at all—is the desire to embrace contradictions, indeed the desire to seek them out the better to play with the possibilities they afford" (6).

Thus, De Quincey's Romantic vision of rhetoric's potential role in "playing with the possibilities" provides a philosophical transition between the eighteenth century's investigation of rhetoric's potential to preserve community through aesthetic appeals to the imagination and nineteenth-century arguments for an aesthetic ideal capable of transcending the harsh certainties of a society dominated by commercial interests. As the nineteenth century moves forward, theorists such as Thomas Carlyle, John Ruskin, Matthew Arnold, Pater, Vernon Lee, and Wilde sustain De Quincey's inquiry into the potential of language to effect cultural revitalization. Although these writers use a vocabulary that differs from that found in texts that have been incorporated in the rhetorical canon, they deserve a place in rhetorical history.

The fact that De Quincey's perspective has generally been ignored, dismissed, or derided holds interesting implications for rhetorical historiography. The small body of scholarship on De Quincey's rhetorical theory can be accounted for in several ways. The construction of the rhetorical canon has historically been based on a fairly narrow definition of rhetoric. As a number of scholars note, this presumption has favored theoretical treatments of rhetoric focused on civic judgment and has generally excluded rhetorical practices, particularly those that have deviated from the goal of rational judgment about clearly defined civic issues. Although belletristic rhetorical theories technically expand rhetoric's province to include more varied types of discourse, the canon has traditionally included only the theories that describe those practices, not the practices themselves. In De Quincey's case, the choice of writing an excursive essay that emphasizes rhetoric as an intellectual and stylistic practice aimed at exploring multiple possibilities, rather than as a means to arrive at a decision, has caused many rhetoricians to assume that he has no place in the field.

The limited scholarship on De Quincey's rhetoric is evident in bibliographies of writings about De Quincey. H. O. Dendurent's *Thomas De Quincey: A Reference Guide* provides an annotated bibliography of writings on De Quincey between 1821 and 1975, listed by year. This thorough and comprehensive listing includes scattered articles focused on his writings about rhetoric. Another source on writings about De Quincey is Julian North's *De Quincey Reviewed: Thomas De Quincey's Critical Reception, 1821–1994*. North stresses that her intention is not to discover "the 'true' De Quincey" but to offer insight into "the diverse responses he has elicited over the years and the fluctuations in his critical reputation" (1). Both of these sources therefore provide not only an accessible catalogue of scholarly treatments of De Quincey's work but also illustrate the ebbs and flows of critical interest in De Quincey, which both directly and indirectly has a bearing on the reception of his theories about rhetoric.

The reviews by both Dendurent and North reveal that De Quincey's thoughts on rhetoric received little attention during his lifetime and the years immediately following. As mentioned earlier, most of the early critical attention to De Quincey's work focused on the *Confessions*, as well as other autobiographical writings. North notes that although De Quincey's autobiographical works are generally accepted as having literary merit, the critiques of his scholarly writings are much more divided. In tracing the progress of these critiques, she notes a pattern of mounting controversy in the decades following De Quincey's death. North states that "in the 1840s and 50s there was still relatively little commentary on these aspects of De Quincey's work, but that little tended to be favourable" (120). She adds that "the 1860s and 70s saw some increase of interest in De Quincey as literary theorist, critic, and scholar, and a larger measure of praise" (121) but adds that "less enthusiastic responses" were also beginning to come to the fore. North quotes, in particular, one of a reviewer's comments on De Quincey's

Selections Grave and Gay, the reviewer puts forth a rather surprisingly strident attack in an 1863 volume of *British Quarterly Review* against De Quincey's theory on moral grounds: "No man could have written about Rhetoric as Mr. De Quincey has written, who had any proper sense of moral obligation, or any comprehension of either the perspicacity of persons *not* addicted to opium, or of their average sense of right and wrong" (qtd. in North 122).

On the other hand, De Quincey's notion of rhetoric did hold some interest in the late nineteenth century. David Masson highlighted De Quincey's intellectual strength, with a particular focus on his work in "Rhetoric," "Style," and "Language," which Masson perceived as having "superseded Addison, Johnson, Jeffrey and Whately" (North 122). In addition, noted nineteenth-century educator Fred Newton Scott published an 1893 edition of De Quincey's "Style," "Rhetoric," "Language," and "The English Language." In the preface to that text, Scott writes, "Rhetoric, in spite of the attention which in every age of the world has been earnestly bestowed upon it, is probably to-day the most belated of the sciences. For this the text-books must to some extent be held responsible. They all, good and bad, have a depressing air of fixity and finality" (iii). Scott explains himself as offering the publication of De Quincey's work, along with that of George Henry Lewes and Herbert Spencer, in recognition of the fact that "old prejudices are in process of breaking down and must ultimately be swept away" (iii).

In spite of Scott's endorsement of the value of De Quincey's work in rhetoric, that work met with strong criticism during the early decades of the twentieth century. In part, this criticism was grounded in the assumptions of rhetoric's "fixity and finality" that Scott decries. In spite of his insistence that his thoughts on rhetoric participate in an Aristotelian succession, De Quincey's Romantic vision of rhetoric grounded in subjectivity and indeterminacy differs markedly from major strains in the Western rhetorical tradition. In addition, De Quincey's writings on rhetoric feature the lack of coherence that is fundamental to his notion of how rhetoric functions. This pattern goes against another established feature of traditional Western rhetorical treatises, which are generally at least somewhat systematic.

Widely ranging judgments can be seen in more recent scholarship on De Quincey's rhetoric. Much of the scholarly discussion of De Quincey's rhetoric centers less upon the question of what he says than on the issue of whether there is value in asking that question in the first place. Wilbur Samuel Howell's "De Quincey on Science, Rhetoric, and Poetry" contains one of the most strongly stated arguments that De Quincey's rhetoric holds no value at all. The immediate purpose of Howell's essay is to provide a response to Charles Sears Baldwin's comparison between De Quincey's concept of literature of knowledge and literature of power to Aristotle's treatment of rhetoric and poetics. Howell's argument that there is no similarity between the two is grounded in a strong preference for Aristotle, whose theory he depicts as containing a clarity and precision lacking in De Quincey (10).

A similar position is advanced by Rene Wellek, whom North describes as De Quincey's "chief detractor" (124). In "De Quincey's Status in the History of Ideas," published two years before Howell's article, Wellek characterizes De Quincey as an unoriginal thinker, a "spinner of dreams" (270) whose ideas are essentially inconsequential (252–55). Wellek's sweeping conclusion that "De Quincey's use of rhetoric is rightly forgotten" (269) can be interpreted as a dismissal of both his theory and practice, which could be seen as appropriate given that the two are so strongly connected. Wellek's critiques of De Quincey's intellectual depth and originality are carried forward in various ways in the work of other scholars.

While the voices of these scholars have likely reinforced the standing assumption that De Quincey has no viable place in "the rhetorical tradition," others have offered arguments that support De Quincey's significance as a rhetorical theorist and practitioner. In "Thomas De Quincey in a Revisionist History of Rhetoric," William A. Covino contrasts De Quincey's open-ended approach to rhetoric with the prescriptive approach taken by the more influential Hugh Blair. He describes De Quincey's work as significant in its emphasis on rhetoric as an intellectual process, an approach that allows for the possibility that comes from open-ended inquiry. For Covino, De Quincey's rhetoric participates in the revisionary work of other early modern writers such as Montaigne, Vico, and Hume, representing an example of the "multiple perspectives" (122) available in rhetoric's unfolding history. Covino describes this exploration in positive terms as a feature of De Quincey's willingness to define rhetoric in terms that depart from reaching immediate resolution: "[R]hetoric fully exercised does not encourage blind adherence, but rather, full participation in the art of wondering, 'that state of tense exertion on the part of both auditor and performer'" (126). Covino further explores De Quincey's place in the rhetorical tradition in "Phantastic Palimpsests: Thomas De Quincey and the Magical Composing Imagination," where he considers De Quincey's role in the restoration of the links among rhetoric, magic, and the imagination following the seventeenth-century union of rhetoric with scientific fact.

Lawrence D. Needham shares Covino's sense that De Quincey's work deserves further attention in accounts of the history of rhetoric, but he offers a different characterization of how De Quincey's position relates to other rhetorical traditions. In contrast with the frequent claim that De Quincey's interpretation of Aristotle is simply mistaken, a view argued at some length by Masson, the editor of De Quincey's *Collected Writings*, Needham acknowledges, "Surprisingly, some of De Quincey's views on Aristotelian rhetoric are supportable and cannot be dismissed out of hand" (50). However, he notes that De Quincey's subtle alteration of particular Aristotelian principles has a significant impact on his overall conception of rhetoric, an alteration that De Quincey acknowledges to some extent in describing his work as based on a "suggestion derived" from Aristotle ("Rhetoric" 83). Needham identifies an important example of De Quincey's departure from strict parameters of Aristotelian thought in his decision to convert rhetoric's task from the discovery of means of persuasion "in each particular case" to support "any given thesis," a phrase that emphasizes the internal structure of the text over rhetorical context. Needham aptly observes that this shift provides a foundation for De Quincey's view that rhetoric should be detached from a concern with practical civic affairs, a point that "signals his understanding of, and participation in, another line of the rhetorical tradition" (51), declamation. Needham points out that De Quincey's elaborate rhetorical performances invite the attention that he might otherwise have missed due to the limits surrounding nineteenth-century publication—a situation of which De Quincey was obviously aware.

The possibilities embedded in De Quincey's theory of style and its influence are explored by Secor in "The Legacy of Nineteenth-Century Style Theory." Secor traces a number of contemporary assumptions about style to the nineteenth century and identifies De Quincey as a major influence on nineteenth-century developments in style. While she acknowledges that De Quincey's essay on style is a "highly discursive and unsystematic treatment of the subject," she maintains that most of the ideas about style that develop later in the century "can be seen as filling in details on De Quincey's outline map" (79). According to Secor, De Quincey's contributions to style theory include the notion that an "unself-conscious" style can provide a solid foundation for further awareness of style (79), a rejection of "the hierarchical view of style" (79), an assessment of the varied functions of style (81), and the distinction between the "mechanology" and "organology" of style, which facilitates a careful study of the precise relationship between grammar and style distinct from its aesthetic qualities (80). Secor's identification of significant features of De Quincey's dense and complex theory and recognition of the later manifestation of these ideas in the work of subsequent theorists usefully contributes to our understanding of De Quincey's role in both nineteenth-century and contemporary understandings of style.

Rex Veeder also positions De Quincey's thought within his own cultural context, as he includes De Quincey in a list of distinguished figures who develop what he describes as "rhetorical tenets of the British Romantics" ("Expressive" 101). While Veeder acknowledges that the Romantics "did not develop a detailed and systematic rhetoric," he adds that "they did not . . . flinch from arguing about discourse and education—the two primary elements in rhetorical study" ("Expressive" 100). Veeder's description of key assumptions underlying Romantic principles of rhetoric closely parallels many features of De Quincey's work, and he refers specifically to De Quincey's "middle species of composition" in delineating the Romantic view that "personal discourse in journals, notebooks, letters, personal essays, and literature is an essential and primary rhetorical activity" ("Expressive" 102–3). Veeder's "Romantic Rhetoric and the Rhetorical Tradition" identifies De Quincey's essay on rhetoric as "a good starting point for a discussion of the British Romantics' view of rhetoric" (301). The broad scope of Romantic rhetoric outlined in that article does not allow for a thorough investigation of De Quincey's particular views, but Veeder provides an argument that usefully demonstrates links between Romanticism and rhetorical history and provides insight into De Quincey's place in that intellectual domain.

Weldon B. Durham's "Elements of Thomas De Quincey's Rhetoric" presents a close reading of "Rhetoric." Durham maintains that scholars who have attempted to impose a strict sense of order on De Quincey's essays pertaining to rhetoric have created confusion about De Quincey's views, warning that "we need to avoid hastily attributing coherence to De Quincey's essays" (240). He describes De Quincey as perceiving "rhetoric to be a limited and exclusive class of literature whose defining characteristic is a certain kind of intellectual pleasure" (246). Durham avoids adopting a position with respect to De Quincey's precise place in rhetoric's history but suggests that the careful analysis of De Quincey's "key terms" should be seen as an important first step in developing a "comprehensive synopsis and evaluation of his theories of rhetoric" (248).

Frederick Burwick's introduction to the 1967 collection of De Quincey's *Essays on Rhetoric* provides a useful overview of De Quincey's theory, including his emphasis on the unity of style and meaning. Burwick argues, "De Quincey's signal contribution to the history of rhetoric is that he brought together for the first time the principal elements of Scottish associationism and German aesthetics" (xiii). As Burwick notes, De Quincey's orientation is belletristic rather than oratorical (xi), but this is in keeping with the thinking of the rhetorical theorists in the generation immediately preceding his own. Burwick states that De Quincey builds on Henry Home, Lord Kames's perspectives on natural style and rhetorical invention, engages with the views of Scottish rhetoricians with respect to the importance of sincere feelings, and adapts classical thought in defining decorum as the "expression of genuine conviction or genuine passion" (xxxv). Although Burwick acknowledges that De Quincey's "adaptations draw only from individual details and there is no attempt to consolidate the details in a systematic whole" (xlii), it is nevertheless worthwhile to take note of strains of influence that connect De Quincey to lines of thought that fall within the mainstream of rhetorical history.

Burwick focuses on other aspects of De Quincey's work elsewhere. In "Nexus in De Quincey's Theory of Language," Burwick examines intersections between De Quincey's notions of the "organology" and "mechanology" of style, as he argues that De Quincey conceives of "organic" language use as emerging naturally through style's mechanical components. In Burwick's view, this process mirrors that by which the intellect acquires substantial knowledge through the interplay between the technical structures of language, the stylistic play that lies at the heart of rhetorical practice, and the emotive language of eloquence (introduction, xxiv). In *Thomas De Quincey: Knowledge and Power*, Burwick examines how De Quincey's use of literary categories reflects fundamental principles in his thought.

Like Durham and Burwick, Hoyt H. Hudson sets out to acquire a more complete understanding of De Quincey's thought, in spite of what he identifies as the inconsistency that pervades De Quincey's discussion of rhetoric. He closely examines the relationship between invention and style in De Quincey's work, describing them as "an inner and an outer activity" (205) that are related components of the process of creating meaning through language. Hudson credits De Quincey with unique skill in describing "the organic union" of style and invention (206). He also finds in De Quincey's approach to rhetoric a connection to the epideictic tradition; in concert with Needham, he stresses De Quincey's contribution in developing a rhetoric based not in a prescriptive approach to language use but in dynamic practice (209). Although Hudson shows a strong interest in De Quincey's theory, he acknowledges that "when one attempts to go further and to ascertain De Quincey's concepts of rhetoric, eloquence, and style, and the interrelation of these, one is baffled by the author's continual discursiveness and occasional inconsistency" (199).

Paul M. Talley shares the interest of other scholars in the intricate links between De Quincey's conceptions of invention and style. In "De Quincey on Persuasion, Invention, and Style," Talley argues that De Quincey's notion of invention focuses directly on persuasion rather than discovery (243). He describes De Quincey as creating a rhetoric that persuades through the "building of attitudes" (245), and he explores at some length the way in which De Quincey outlines the function of language in persuading through its effect on the audience, noting De Quincey's contention that the artificiality of rhetoric provides the means for intellectual pleasure that overcomes the lack of certain knowledge about or emotional connection to a particular subject. Talley also supports the interpretation of De Quincey's artifice as moving the rhetor and audience toward meaningful knowledge: "Because neither the premises nor the line of reasoning can be validated by scientific demonstration or by 'spontaneous feelings,' both must be made attractive by 'artificial aids.' . . . They are artificial in the sense that they are the rhetorician's observable art, not in the sense that they are superficial embellishment" (249). He conceives of De Quincey's essay on style as constructively expanding his rhetorical theory, concluding that pleasure can be seen as a "necessary means to persuasion" (250), with style serving a function in the development of ethical and logical proof (253).

In contrast with Talley, Frederick W. Haberman sees De Quincey's rhetoric as entirely detached from invention directed toward persuasion. Instead, he argues that De Quincey's rhetoric "turns thought inward upon itself" (194), as the "intellectual play" associated with rhetoric should be seen as directed toward "mental titillation" (195). He perceives an internal conflict between the orientation of "Rhetoric," which he interprets as entirely uninterested in the question of audience, and "Style," a text in which audience is central. This interpretation leads to Haberman's provocative conclusion that De Quincey's rhetorical theory actually consists of two theories, one involving an emphasis on intellectual play that De Quincey considered to be his own province and the other focused on a more traditional conception of persuasion, which De Quincey was willing to advance for the benefit of the public at large.

John E. Jordan's introduction to *De Quincey as Critic* offers a useful overview of De Quincey's approach to criticism, including an exploration of the distinction between De Quincey's theoretical interest in criticism as subject matter and his approach to the practice of criticism grounded in his interest in appropriateness (36). Jordan also examines De Quincey's literary criticism, which has been characterized in widely different ways, in *Thomas De Quincey,*

Literary Critic: His Method and Achievement. In one section of the book, Jordan examines how De Quincey's ideas about rhetoric contribute to his criticism of the writings and oratory of historical figures and contemporaries.

These scholars offer insight into De Quincey's rhetorical theory at least in part through examining it in relation to other perspectives on rhetoric. Others pursue an understanding of specific elements of De Quincey's thinking about rhetoric, which can be a challenging task in itself. While this scholarship is not extensive, it nevertheless reveals the complexity of De Quincey's rhetorical and critical theories and the varied interpretations that they leave open to scholars.

Josephine McDonagh explores the political position De Quincey establishes through his writing. Her interest in how De Quincey's attempt to order knowledge reflects and resists the changing knowledge bases of his society holds value for an understanding of his approach to rhetoric. McDonagh focuses on the complexity embedded in De Quincey's authorship: "The economy of knowledge that we will find in De Quincey's work is one formulated by a commercial writer, with High Tory sympathies and a nostalgia for Romanticism, working at a time of extreme social rupture as political and class allegiances shifted in response to political reform, industrialization, and the expansion of markets across the world" (6). Drawing upon Foucault, McDonagh examines the ways in which different discourses of power can be seen as organizing principles for De Quincey's work.

Julianne Smith looks at De Quincey's theory through yet another lens, as she argues that De Quincey, along with Margaret Oliphant, should be seen as playing an important role in altering perceptions of rhetoric in Victorian periodical culture. She argues that De Quincey's emphasis on the interiority of writing, appreciation for women's style, and interest in imaginative discourse helped to create a path through which nineteenth-century women could acquire a rhetorical presence, whether or not that was his actual intention.

Many texts examine De Quincey's participation in wider conversations pertaining to language and publication in the nineteenth century. Among these works are Oliphant's *Annals of a Publishing House: William Blackwood and His Sons*, which provides an overview of what Oliphant depicts as De Quincey's stormy relationship with one of his major publishers. Robert Morrison's "William Blackwood and the Dynamics of Success," published in *Print Culture and the Blackwood Tradition, 1805–1930*, an anthology of essays dealing with the history of *Blackwood's Magazine*, lists De Quincey as one of the writers who contributed to Blackwood's effort to make the magazine "one of the most controversial and highly marketable publications of the day" (22). Tony Crowley describes De Quincey as participating in developing conversations about the history of language. He argues that De Quincey's "The English Language" (1839) is particularly "important in that it characterizes much of the contemporary thinking about language in England, and indicates the future direction of such work" (294).

These views suggest that engaging in the effort to understand De Quincey's notion of rhetoric holds the potential for frustration as well as surprising insight. However, even if De Quincey's treatment of rhetoric cannot be seen as linear or coherent in the traditional sense, De Quincey's thought circulates around particular themes that form patterns reflecting his view of how language effects social vitality through the creative agency of the individual. De Quincey's belief in language's function to express individual creativity and to enhance public consciousness accounts for his emphasis on rhetoric as intellectual play, which has provided an important point of focus in the efforts of many scholars to define De Quincey's relationship to the rhetorical tradition. Burwick highlights this feature in his summary statement that De Quincey's "art of rhetoric is addressed to the ends of intellectual pleasure through the management of language" (introduction, xxxvi). Durham seems to support this point of view but is more negative in his assessment that "De Quincey considered rhetoric to be a limited and exclusive class of literature whose defining characteristic is a certain kind of intellectual pleasure" (246).

For De Quincey, the rhetorician's skill involves the use of external resources that artificially guide the audience toward perceiving a question in a particular way. Yet, several critics argue that De Quincey's insistence upon a fanciful spirit and playful language should not be interpreted as an unwillingness to deal with serious subjects. In his discussion of De Quincey's "Rhetoric," Jordan argues that for De Quincey, "it is clear that rhetoric may deal with serious and important topics, but they must not be questions of the law courts or the fora, not subjects susceptible of definite proof or demanding immediate action" (*Thomas De Quincey* 216). Hudson agrees that De Quincey's emphasis on "intellectual play" does not entirely eschew engagement with significant social issues, noting that "[w]hat is needed to convert rhetorical play into earnest is a persuasive purpose" (202), and later adds, "Even when he [De Quincey] thought of it as fanciful play, the objects played with . . . were ideas" (203). Thus, De Quincey's "fanciful play" constitutes a turn toward intellectual exploration grounded in subjectivity but nevertheless directed toward engagement with an audience and an external world of ideas. Yet, this engagement ironically turns back in upon itself. Barry Milligan's "Brunonianism, Radicalism, and 'The Pleasures of Opium'" discusses De Quincey's writing as generating opportunities to explore multiple possibilities, as Milligan introduces the article with a discussion of "De Quincey's elusively ironic, proto-deconstructive sensibility" (46).

In light of the oppositions that pervade De Quincey's work, it is perhaps not surprising to read Howell's assessment that De Quincey's idea of rhetoric is "so far divorced from actual human experience, so completely devoid of connection with the urgent issues of politics and law, that we can only wonder why De Quincey would think it worth while for Aristotle or any serious-minded person to bother with it in any theoretical or practical way" (3). Howell is certainly accurate in describing De Quincey's theory as lacking in practicality—which is precisely De Quincey's aim. While he definitely departs from Aristotle's assumed aim of arriving at public judgment, De Quincey does achieve his stated goal of exploring the consequences of Aristotle's notion that rhetoric involves examining issues that have no definitive correct answer. De Quincey takes the issue of probability to an extreme, exemplifying his claim that Aristotle "threw the whole stress upon finding such arguments for any given thesis as, without positively proving or disproving it, should give it a colourable support" ("Rhetoric" 85–86). In arguing that the "real governing law of Aristotle's procedure" lies in finding the plausible rather than the true, "not which the understanding can solemnly approve and abide by—but the very opposite to this; one which it can submit to for a moment, and countenance as within the limits of the plausible" ("Rhetoric" 86), De Quincey reinterprets classical notions concerning rhetoric's relationship to probability for an age increasingly doubtful about the availability of certain truth. In the process, he recaptures for a modern context earlier classical traditions grounded in rhetorical practice that is not entirely defined by system. As Hudson notes, De Quincey "points us away from that sort of rhetoric which is largely an *ex post facto* critical apparatus, emphasizing nomenclature, classification, and theme *correction* to the older discipline (never wholly extinct, but certainly under a cloud for some generations) which was largely a mode of procedure for the *preparation* of a theme or speech" (209; original emphasis). While De Quincey's articulation of a dialogic rhetoric formed through performance may confound scholars searching for clear guidelines to rhetorical practice, his commitment to revitalizing and restoring the link between invention and style can be seen as participating in long-standing conversations concerning the dynamic process of rhetorical production.

Given his fundamental conception of rhetoric, it is fitting that De Quincey's exposition of his rhetorical theory contains unresolved conflicts. In fact, conflict lies at the heart of De Quincey's theory; although he adopts a strong critical stance toward industrial society, he ultimately generates what Julianne Smith describes as "a rhetoric of authorship in a way scarcely possible before the nineteenth-century industrialization of print and the spread of literacy" (40). This perspective on De Quincey is in keeping with Walter J. Ong's general observation that in spite of the apparent opposition between Romanticism and technology, the two can actually be seen as "mirror images of each other, both being products of man's dominance over nature and of the noetic abundance which had been created by chirographic and typographic techniques of storing and retrieving knowledge" (264). In Ong's view, then, Romanticism can be seen as critiquing the very mechanization upon which originality depends; the Romantic rejection of the commonplace reflects a desire to replace the collective knowledge of oral traditions with a yearning for the original and unknown promised by print. The phenomenon Ong describes is certainly evident in De Quincey, whose dependence on print not only relates to his livelihood but also to his theoretical emphasis on inventional processes that rely upon writing and on rhetoric defined in terms of the individual's sharing of an internal subjectivity. The internal conflict and lack of coherence in De Quincey's rhetoric embody the ironic opposition that lies at the heart of his rhetorical theory and practice. Through the course of his essays, De Quincey reveals rhetoric to be one of many subjects that can be seen in many different ways, with supporting ideas in which "the affirmative and the negative are both true" ("Rhetoric" 91).

Even a brief overview of writings about De Quincey's ideas about rhetoric reveals that the complexity that underlies De Quincey's work yields the possibility of varied interpretations. While both Howell and Wellek would likely see this point as supporting their rejection of De Quincey as a theorist and thinker, De Quincey himself might not be troubled by scholarly conflicts about his work. It seems entirely in keeping with the position he adopts to see that one scholar could convincingly argue for the importance of a concept in De Quincey's work that another scholar finds to be entirely absent from it. In the process of advancing their very different views on De Quincey's thought, scholars have illustrated what appear to be central premises of De Quincey's rhetorical theory: rhetoric inevitably engages with questions in which there is no certain knowledge, and it does so in a way that finds delight in varied possibilities. In this respect, De Quincey's writings on rhetoric, as well as critical responses to those writings, can be seen as successfully representing the premises he articulates in his essays.

De Quincey's affinity with Romanticism has undoubtedly contributed to his relative obscurity in British rhetorical history. In describing the abrupt shift from the Enlightenment to the twentieth century in most accounts of the history of rhetoric, Don H. Bialostosky and Lawrence D. Needham argue that the nineteenth century has been neglected due to the implicit agreement among rhetorical scholars "[t]hat rhetoric declined as Romanticism rose" (introduction 1). The current volume, in part, reflects an effort to participate in the conversation that Bialostosky and Needham, along with Veeder and others, have initiated. De Quincey unquestionably departs from classical views of rhetoric as political oratory in advancing a claim for rhetoric as an evolving process that provides a vehicle for the creative expression of the individual. De Quincey's radical revision of the tradition merits the attention of rhetorical scholars, both because of its unique features and because it manifests the dynamic relationship between rhetoric and culture that continues to be evident at each stage of rhetoric's history. De Quincey's insistence that privacy, imagination, and uncertainty are central aspects of rhetorical production also connects in interesting ways with contemporary efforts to argue for rhetorical alternatives to theories that confine rhetoric to public practices that are accessible to only a few people. Of course, De Quincey's enactment of intellectual play, like other versions of Romantic genius, can be seen as exclusive in its own right, but it does at least provide different parameters for rhetorical practice than those that have obtained throughout much of rhetoric's history, which provides an opportunity for new possibilities for conceiving of what rhetoric might entail.

De Quincey's position in the history of rhetoric provides an excellent example of how the construction of history inevitably reflects the values of different generations of scholars. While subjective interpretation is indeed an unavoidable part of historiography, De Quincey's example illustrates the gaps that are created when accounts of rhetorical history are too much guided by judgments of the value of a particular rhetorical approach rather than by an appreciation of rhetoric's complexity as people adapt to specific cultural circumstances. Contemporary scholars who appreciate the value of indeterminacy may find De Quincey's dialogic rhetoric more appealing than scholars in the generation of Howell and Wellek, but De Quincey's place in rhetorical history should not rest entirely on the extent to which his thought is or is not compatible with the ideas of the scholars who study his work. De Quincey's contribution to rhetorical history lies not in answering timeless questions that have been passed down for generations but in posing questions pertinent to his own age—an age experiencing changes that were of concern to De Quincey and his contemporaries. His unique interplay of tradition and innovation in advancing his ideas provides insight into the dynamic presence of rhetoric in an age in which "the pressures for change were enclosed within established and familiar boundaries" (Price 12).

In addition to understanding the significance of specific elements of De Quincey's thought, the study of De Quincey's rhetoric also holds the value of expanding understanding of the subtle and dramatic revisions that take place as rhetoric responds to different historical and cultural moments. In addition, it calls into question assumptions about the limits and possibilities of rhetoric as a discipline. Bialostosky and Needham state that the purpose of their anthology on Romantic rhetorics is to facilitate the "recognition of and inquiry into rhetoric in British Romantic literature, but it holds that such recognition is best achieved not by fixing in our mind's eye a single idea of rhetoric. . . . Recognition and inquiry are best cultivated, we believe, by familiarizing ourselves with the family resemblances that connect and separate concurrent rhetorical enterprises and link them to others over time in 'traditions' or genealogies" (introduction 2). Tracing the genealogies of De Quincey's rhetoric illuminates its participation in ongoing efforts to explore rhetoric's potential as production, display, and the means for intellectual growth through creative invention.

De Quincey's Romantic emphasis on possibility, enacted through dialogic rhetoric, offers a vision of rhetoric's role in the creative revitalization central to many eighteenth- and nineteenth-century language theorists. It also offers an immediate response to cultural conditions that De Quincey perceived as a threat to the imaginative activity needed for true intellectual growth. His view of rhetoric also offers a useful counter to the public/private binary that has frequently pervaded histories of rhetoric. In "Reconstructing a Rhetoric of the Interior," Thomas S. Frentz writes, "I doubt that the art can flourish as long as rhetoric-as-public-address remains its sole theoretical possibility" (88), and argues that rhetoric's vitality can be preserved through sharing Carl Jung's recognition "that addressing others presupposes that we are in the process of addressing ourselves" (88). De Quincey's dialogic approach provides an important model of rhetorical theory and practice that intricately connects public and private, in the process avoiding either a strict alignment with rhetoric's traditional civic function or a retreat into an entirely private world of unexamined truth.

De Quincey's work has remarkable significance for a rhetorical history that offers alternative ways of theorizing, practicing, and teaching rhetoric and writing. De Quincey gives an important response to the question of "what a dialogical rhetoric, might be" (Zappen 6). In offering this vision of rhetoric, De Quincey anticipates Charles Schuster's insight that "dialogism is an inherent quality of language; it also seems to me to represent a basic model for epistemology, for how we come to know" (4). De Quincey's insistence on the capacity of language to promote intellectual development through an exploration of multiple possibilities highlights the presence of alternative strains in rhetorical history that investigate rhetoric's complex epistemic possibilities, countering what has at times been restricted to a focus on the monological quest to lead an audience to judgment.

Although De Quincey's rhetoric reflects concerns particular to the early nineteenth century and he makes no claim to pedagogical aims, his perspective holds intriguing insights for contemporary teachers of rhetoric and composition. His claims for rhetoric provide one point of entry for pursuing the benefits Bialostosky identifies for those who engage with dialogical criticism: "As readers sophisticated by an art of dialogics, then, we would self-consciously represent the voice-ideas of others and involve others in dialogues they had not anticipated, but we would also self-consciously expect unexpected replies and foresee unforeseen uses of our own words and ourselves by others" ("Dialogics" 791). His rhetorical theory and practice also provide early models for the pedagogical project of a dialogism that Kay Halasek promotes for the composition classroom: "A dialogical understanding of reality in fact mandates that compositionists recognize that knowledge, and therefore pedagogy, is constructed from multiple and conflicting knowledge claims, and that purist ideological frames limit understanding" (177). De Quincey's strategic use of irony that resists certainty and closure, and his explicit recognition of the intellectual value that comes from such a practice, provide a heritage for more contemporary efforts to pursue multiple voices and positions in teaching and theorizing.

In writing about evolutions in language, De Quincey argues that some changes are better than others but that it is a mistake "to find a disease in the pains of growth" ("Language" 246). To some extent, De Quincey's reputation has suffered from those who have resisted "the pains of growth," and the current volume represents an effort to challenge that view. Certainly, De Quincey's theory is startling in its rejection of the civic mission that many of his contemporaries had assumed to be rhetoric's primary domain. De Quincey deserves attention for precisely that reason, as he offers a vision of rhetoric that emphasizes invention rather than closure, anticipating later insights about the value of discourse whose aim is "not to reach agreement but to sustain the process of exchange itself" (Clark 8). De Quincey's ideas, like those of many other theorists and practitioners who have been placed outside the mainstream of the rhetorical canon, provide a valuable infusion of energy to the discipline—and a reminder that rhetoric's vitality comes from its capacity to respond to cultural change in ways that are endlessly varied and complex.

WORKS CITED AND REFERENCED

INDEX

Works Cited and Referenced

Agnew, Lois. "The Civic Function of Taste: A Re-Assessment of Hugh Blair's Rhetorical Theory." *Rhetoric Society Quarterly* 28.2 (1998): 25–36. Print.

———. *Outward, Visible Propriety: Stoic Philosophy and Eighteenth-Century British Rhetorics*. Columbia: U of South Carolina P, 2008. Print.

———. "Rhetorical Style and the Formation of Character: Ciceronian *Ethos* in Thomas Wilson's *Arte of Rhetorique*." *Rhetoric Review* 17.1 (1998): 93–106. Print.

Altick, Richard D. *The English Common Reader: A Social History of the Mass Reading Public, 1800–1900*. Chicago: U of Chicago P, 1957. Print.

Aristotle. *On Rhetoric: A Theory of Civic Discourse*. Trans. George A. Kennedy. New York: Oxford UP, 1991.

Ashton, T. S. "The Industrial Revolution." *Backgrounds to British Romantic Literature*. Ed. Karl Kroeber. San Francisco: Chandler, 1968. 63–79. Print.

Bacon, Francis. "Of Friendship." *Essays, Civil and Moral*. Vol. 3, part 1. The Harvard Classics. New York: Collier, 1909–14. Bartleby.com, 2001. Web. 24 Sept. 2007. <http://www.bartleby.com/3/1/27.html>.

Baird Smith, Florence (De Quincey). [Correspondence between Mrs. Bairdsmith and John Blackwood relating to an article in Blackwood's magazine for December 1877 on De Quincey]." Item 26, MS Eng 1009, Thomas De Quincey papers, Houghton Library, Harvard College Library, Harvard University.

———. "[Correspondence between Mrs. Bairdsmith and the editor of Macmillan's magazine]." London, [23 June] 1890, 8 p., MS. in the hand of a copyist. Item 27, MS Eng 1009, Thomas De Quincey papers, Houghton Library, Harvard College Library, Harvard University.

———. "[Correspondence between Mrs. Bairdsmith, Messrs A & C Black and David Masson relating to Masson's edition of *De Quincey's Works*]." London, 1886–89, MS transcript, 35f. Item 27, MS Eng 1009, Thomas De Quincey papers, Houghton Library, Harvard College Library, Harvard University.

Bakhtin, M. M. *The Dialogic Imagination: Four Essays*. Trans. Carl Emerson and Michael Holquist. Ed. Michael Holquist. Austin: U of Texas P, 1981. Print.

———. "Discourse in the Novel." Bakhtin, *Dialogic Imagination* 259–422.

———. "Epic and Novel." Bakhtin, *Dialogic Imagination* 3–40.

Bialostosky, Don H. "Dialogics as an Art of Discourse in Literary Criticism." *PMLA* 101.5 (1986): 788–97. Print.

———. *Wordsworth, Dialogics, and the Practice of Criticism*. Cambridge: Cambridge UP, 1992. Print.

Bialostosky, Don H., and Lawrence D. Needham. Introduction. Bialostosky and Needham, *Rhetorical Traditions* 1–8.

———, eds. *Rhetorical Traditions and British Romantic Literature*. Bloomington: Indiana UP, 1995. Print.

Blair, Hugh. *Lectures on Rhetoric and Belles Lettres*. 1783. Ed. and with an introduction by Linda Ferreira-Buckley and S. Michael Halloran. Carbondale: Southern Illinois UP, 2005. Print.

Buckley, Jerome H. *The Victorian Temper: A Study in Literary Culture*. London: Routledge, 1966. Print.

Burwick, Frederick. Introduction. Burwick, *Selected Essays* xi–xlviii.

———. "Nexus in De Quincey's Theory of Language." *Thomas De Quincey Bicentenary Studies*. Ed. and with an introduction by Robert Lance Snyder. Norman: U of Oklahoma P, 1985. 263–78. Print.

———, ed. *Selected Essays on Rhetoric by Thomas De Quincey*. 1967. Carbondale: Southern Illinois UP, 2010. Print. Landmarks in Rhetoric and Public Address Series. General ed. David Potter.

———. *Thomas De Quincey: Knowledge and Power*. Hampshire: Palgrave, 2001. Print.

Camlot, Jason. *Style and the Nineteenth-Century British Critic: Sincere Mannerisms*. Burlington: Ashgate, 2008. Print.

Campbell, George. *The Philosophy of Rhetoric*. 1776. *Philosophy of Rhetoric*. Ed. Lloyd Bitzer. 1963. Carbondale: Southern Illinois UP, 2010. Print.

Carlyle, Thomas. "Letter to Ralph Waldo Emerson." 12 August 1834. *The Correspondence of Thomas Carlyle and Ralph Waldo Emerson, 1834–1872*, Vol. 1. Ed. Charles Eliot Norton. Boston: Ticknor, 1886. 18–26. Print.

———. "Signs of the Times." *Critical and Miscellaneous Essays*. Vol. 2. *The Works of Thomas Carlyle, in 30 Volumes*. 27 vols. Ed. H. D. Traill. New York: Scribner, n.d. 56–82. Print.

Carruthers, Robert. To [Alexander Hay] Japp. Inverness [1877]. 13 p. Item 88, MS Eng 1009, Thomas De Quincey papers, Houghton Library, Harvard College Library, Harvard University.

———. To [Alexander Hay] Japp. 25 March 1877. 2 p. Item 89, MS Eng 1009, Thomas De Quincey papers, Houghton Library, Harvard College Library, Harvard University.

Christensen, Jerome. "The Method of *The Friend*." Bialostosky and Needham, *Rhetorical Traditions* 11–27.

Cicero, Marcus Tullius. *De officiis*. Trans. Walter Miller. London: Heinemann, 1913. Print. Loeb Classical Library Series.

Clark, Gregory. *Dialogue, Dialectic, and Conversation: A Social Perspective on the Function of Writing*. Carbondale: Southern Illinois UP, 1990. Print.

Cody, Sherwin. "De Quincey: Inventor of Modern 'Impassioned Prose.'" 1903. *A Selection from the Best English Essays, Illustrative of the History of English Prose Style*. Freeport: Books for Libraries, 1968. 115–18. Print.

Cohen, Herman. "Hugh Blair's Theory of Taste." *Quarterly Journal of Speech* 44.3 (1958): 265–74. Print.

Coleridge, Samuel Taylor. *Biographia Literaria*. 1817. Ed. George Watson. London: Dent, 1956. Print.

Covino, William A. "Phantastic Palimpsests: Thomas De Quincey and the Magical Composing Imagination." *Composition in Context: Essays in Honor of Donald C. Stewart*. Ed. Ross Winterowd and Vincent Gillespie. Carbondale: Southern Illinois UP, 1994. 169–79. Print.

—. "Thomas De Quincey in a Revisionist History of Rhetoric." *Pre/Text* 4.2 (1983): 121–36. Print.

Crowley, Sharon. "Biting the Hand That Feeds Us: Nineteenth-Century Uses of a Pedagogy of Taste." *Rhetoric, Cultural Studies, and Literacy*. Ed. John Frederick Reynolds. Hillsdale: Erlbaum, 1995. 11–20. Print.

Crowley, Tony. "A History of 'The History of the Language.'" *Language and Communication* 6.4 (1986): 293–303. Print.

Dendurent, H. O. *Thomas De Quincey: A Reference Guide*. Boston: Hall, 1978. Print.

De Quincey, Thomas. "The Affliction of Childhood." De Quincey, *Collected Writings* 1:28–54.

—. [Autograph manuscript notes to James Hogg and sons relating to the proofreading of his *Selections grave and gay*]." 1852–59. 157 pieces, items 116–273, Thomas De Quincey papers, Houghton Library, Harvard College Library, Harvard University.

—. "A Brief Appraisal of the Greek Literature in Its Foremost Pretensions." Burwick, *Selected Essays* 289–341.

—. *The Collected Writings of Thomas De Quincey*. Ed. David Masson. 14 vols. Edinburgh: Black, 1890. Print.

—. *Confessions of an English Opium-Eater*. De Quincey, *Collected Writings* 3:207–472.

—. "Conversation." Burwick, *Selected Essays* 264–88.

—. *A Diary of Thomas De Quincey*. Ed. Horace A. Eaton. London: Douglas, n.d. Written in 1803. Print.

—. "The English Mail-Coach." De Quincey, *Collected Writings* 13:270–330.

—. "First Irish Rebellion of 1798." De Quincey, *Collected Writings* 10:227–48.

—. "French Invasion of Ireland, and Second Rebellion of 1798." De Quincey, *Collected Writings* 11:249–66.

—. "German Studies and Kant in Particular." De Quincey, *Collected Writings* 2:81–109.

—. "Gradual Estrangement from Wordsworth." De Quincey, *Collected Writings* 3:197–206.

—. "I Am Introduced to the Warfare of a Public School." De Quincey, *Collected Writings* 1:149–60.

—. "I Enter the World." De Quincey, *Collected Writings* 1:161–77.

—. "The Lake Poets: William Wordsworth." De Quincey, *Collected Writings* 2:229–302.

—. "The Lake Poets: William Wordsworth and Robert Southey." De Quincey, *Collected Writings* 2:303–47.

—. "Language." Burwick, *Selected Essays* 246–63.

—. "Letters to a Young Man Whose Education Has Been Neglected: Letter III, On Languages." De Quincey, *Collected Writings* 10:33–52.

—. "On Murder Considered as One of the Fine Arts." De Quincey, *Collected Writings* 13:9–124.

—. "Oxford." De Quincey, *Collected Writings* 2:9–78.

—. "Parentage and the Paternal Home." De Quincey, *Collected Writings* 1:17–27.

—. "The Poetry of Pope." De Quincey, *Collected Writings* 11:51–97.

—. "Premature Manhood." De Quincey, *Collected Writings* 1:316–31.

———. "Rhetoric." Burwick, *Selected Essays* 81–133.

———. "Samuel Taylor Coleridge." De Quincey, *Collected Writings* 2:138–225.

———. "The Saracen's Head." De Quincey, *Collected Writings* 2:348–59.

———. "Style." Burwick, *Selected Essays* 134–245.

———. "A Tory's Account of Toryism, Whiggism, and Radicalism." De Quincey, *Collected Writings* 9:313–53.

Devlin, D. D. *De Quincey, Wordsworth, and the Art of Prose*. New York: St. Martin's, 1983. Print.

Dickins, Amanda. "An 'Intercourse of Sentiments' and the Seductions of Virtue: The Role of Conversation in David Hume's Philosophy." *The Concept and Practice of Conversation in the Long Eighteenth Century, 1688–1848*. Ed. Katie Halsey and Jane Slinn. Newcastle: Cambridge, 2007. 20–39. Print.

Durham, Weldon B. "The Elements of Thomas De Quincey's Rhetoric." *Speech Monographs* 37.4 (1970): 240–48. Print.

Eaton, Horace A. Introduction. *A Diary of Thomas De Quincey*. Ed. Horace A. Eaton. London: Douglas, n.d. Print.

Erickson, Lee. *The Economy of Literary Form: English Literature and the Industrialization of Publishing, 1800–1850*. Baltimore: Johns Hopkins UP, 1996. Print.

Farrell, Thomas. *Norms of Rhetorical Culture*. New Haven: Yale UP, 1993. Print.

Ferreira-Buckley, Linda, and S. Michael Halloran. Editor's introduction. *Lectures on Rhetoric and Belles Lettres, by Hugh Blair*. Carbondale: Southern Illinois UP, 2005. xv–liv. Print.

Freedman, Jonathan. *Professions of Taste: Henry James, British Aestheticism, and Commodity Culture*. Stanford: Stanford UP, 1990. Print.

Frentz, Thomas S. "Reconstructing a Rhetoric of the Interior." *Communication Monographs* 60 (1993): 83–89. Print.

Georgia, Jennifer. "The Joys of Social Intercourse: Men, Women, and Conversation in the Eighteenth Century." *The Concept and Practice of Conversation in the Long Eighteenth Century, 1688–1848*. Ed. Katie Halsey and Jane Slinn. Newcastle: Cambridge, 2007. 249–56. Print.

Gilmour, Robin. *The Victorian Period: The Intellectual and Cultural Context of English Literature, 1830–1890*. London: Longman, 1993. Print.

Gorgias. "Encomium of Helen." Trans. George A. Kennedy. *The Rhetorical Tradition: Readings from Classical Times to the Present*. Ed. Patricia Bizzell and Bruce Herzberg. 2nd ed. Boston: Bedford, 2001. 44–46. Print.

Haberman, Frederick W. "De Quincey's Theory of Rhetoric." *Eastern Public Speaking Conference: Papers and Addresses Delivered at the Thirty-First Annual Meeting: March 28, 29, 30, 1940, Washington, D.C.* Ed. Harold F. Harding. New York: Wilson, 1940. 191–203. Print.

Halasek, Kay. *A Pedagogy of Possibility: Bakhtinian Perspectives on Composition Studies*. Carbondale: Southern Illinois UP, 1999. Print.

Halloran, S. Michael. "On the End of Rhetoric, Classical and Modern." *Landmark Essays on Rhetorical Invention in Writing*. Ed. Richard E. Young and Yameng Liu. Davis, CA: Hermagoras, 1994. 79–90. Print.

Heffernan, James A. W. *Wordsworth's Theory of Poetry: The Transforming Imagination*. Ithaca: Cornell UP, 1969. Print.

Horner, Winifred Bryan, and Kerri Morris Barton. "The Eighteenth Century." *The Present State of Scholarship in Historical and Contemporary Rhetoric.* Ed. Winifred Bryan Horner. Columbia: U of Missouri P, 1990. 114–50. Print.

Hough, Graham. *The Last Romantics.* London: Methuen, 1947. Print.

Howell, Wilbur Samuel. "De Quincey on Science, Rhetoric, and Poetry." *Speech Monographs* 13.1 (1946): 1–13. Print.

Hudson, Hoyt H. "De Quincey on Rhetoric and Public Speaking." *Historical Studies of Rhetoric and Rhetoricians.* Ed. Raymond F. Howes. Ithaca: Cornell UP, 1961. 198–214. Print.

Johnson, Nan. *Nineteenth-Century Rhetoric in North America.* Carbondale: Southern Illinois UP, 1991. Print.

Jordan, John E. "Grazing the Brink: De Quincey's Ironies." *Thomas De Quincey Bicentenary Studies.* Ed. and with an introduction by Robert Lance Snyder. Norman: U of Oklahoma P, 1985. 199–212. Print.

———. Introduction. *De Quincey as Critic.* London: Routledge, 1973. 1–48. Print.

———. *Thomas De Quincey, Literary Critic: His Method and Achievement.* Berkeley: U of California P, 1952. Print.

Kelley, Theresa M. "The Case for William Wordsworth: Romantic Invention versus Romantic Genius." Bialostosky and Needham, *Rhetorical Traditions* 122–38.

Kent, Christopher A. "Victorian Periodicals and the Constructing of Victorian Reality." *Victorian Periodicals: A Guide to Research.* Ed. J. Don Vann and Rosemary T. VanArsdel. New York: MLA, 1989. 1–12. Print.

Klancher, Jon P. *The Making of English Reading Audiences, 1790–1832.* Madison: U of Wisconsin P, 1987. Print.

Kroeber, Karl. Introduction. *Backgrounds to British Romantic Literature.* Ed. Karl Kroeber. San Francisco: Chandler, 1968. 1–18. Print.

Leighton, Angela. "De Quincey and Women." *Beyond Romanticism: New Approaches to Texts and Contexts, 1780–1832.* Ed. Stephen Copley and John Whale. London: Routledge, 1992. 160–77. Print.

Lindop, Grevel. *The Opium-Eater: A Life of Thomas De Quincey.* New York: Taplinger, 1981. Print.

Lovejoy, Arthur O. "On the Discrimination of Romanticisms." *English Romantic Poets: Modern Essays in Criticism.* Ed. M. H. Abrams. New York: Oxford UP, 1960. 3–24. Print. Rpt. of "On the Discrimination of Romanticisms." *Essays in the History of Ideas.* Baltimore: Johns Hopkins P, 1948. 228–53.

McDonagh, Josephine. *De Quincey's Disciplines.* Oxford: Clarendon, 1994. Print.

Milligan, Barry. "Brunonianism, Radicalism, and 'The Pleasures of Opium.'" Morrison and Roberts, *Thomas De Quincey* 45–61.

Morrison, Robert. "'Earthquake and Eclipse': Radical Energies and De Quincey's 1821 *Confessions.*" Morrison and Roberts, *Thomas De Quincey* 63–79.

———. *The English Opium-Eater: A Biography of Thomas De Quincey.* New York: Pegasus, 2010. Print.

———. "William Blackwood and the Dynamics of Success," *Print Culture and the Blackwood Tradition, 1805–1930.* Ed. David Finkelstein. Toronto: U of Toronto P, 21–48. Print.

Morrison, Robert, and Daniel Sanjiv Roberts, eds. *Thomas De Quincey: New Theoretical and Critical Directions*. New York: Routledge, 2008. Print.

Needham, Lawrence D. "De Quincey's Rhetoric of Display and *Confessions of an English Opium-Eater*." Bialostosky and Needham, *Rhetorical Traditions* 48–61.

North, Julian. *De Quincey Reviewed: Thomas De Quincey's Critical Reception, 1821–1994*. Columbia: Camden, 1997. Print.

———. "Wooing the Reader: De Quincey, Wordsworth, and Women in *Tait's Edinburgh Magazine*." Morrison and Roberts, *Thomas De Quincey* 99–121.

Oliphant, Margaret. *Annals of a Publishing House: William Blackwood and His Sons*. Vol. 1. Edinburgh: Blackwood, 1897. Print. 3 vols.

Ong, Walter J. *Rhetoric, Romance, and Technology*. Ithaca: Cornell UP, 1971. Print.

Osborne, John W. *The Silent Revolution: The Industrial Revolution in England as a Source of Cultural Change*. New York: Scribner, 1970. Print.

Pater, Walter. *Plato and Platonism: A Series of Lectures*. 1893. London: Macmillan, 1928. Print.

Peacham, Henry. *The Garden of Eloquence*. 1577. 2nd ed. 1593. Ed. and with an introduction by William G. Crane. Gainesville: Scholars', 1954. Print.

Pilcher, Donald. "The Regency Style." *Backgrounds to British Romantic Literature*. Ed. Karl Kroeber. San Francisco: Chandler, 1968. 169–78. Print.

Price, Richard. *British Society, 1680–1880: Dynamism, Containment, and Change*. Cambridge: Cambridge UP, 1999. Print.

Richards, I. A. *Coleridge on Imagination*. Bloomington: Indiana UP, 1960. Print.

Robbins, Ruth. "Vernon Lee: Decadent Woman?" *Fin de Siècle/Fin du Globe: Fears and Fantasies of the Late Nineteenth Century*. New York: St. Martin's, 1992. 139–61. Print.

Roberts, Daniel Sanjiv. "'Mix(ing) a Little with Alien Natures': Biblical Orientalism in De Quincey." Morrison and Roberts, *Thomas De Quincey* 19–43.

Russett, Margaret. *De Quincey's Romanticism: Canonical Minority and the Forms of Transmission*. Cambridge: Cambridge UP, 1997. Print.

Rzepka, Charles J. *Sacramental Commodities: Gift, Text, and the Sublime in De Quincey*. Amherst: U of Massachusetts P, 1995. Print.

Sackville-West, Edward. *A Flame in Sunlight: The Life and Work of Thomas De Quincey*. London: Cassell, 1936. Print.

Schuster, Charles I. "Mikhail Bakhtin as Rhetorical Theorist." *Landmark Essays on Bakhtin, Rhetoric, and Writing*. Ed. Frank Farmer. Mahwah: Erlbaum, 1998. 1–14. Print. Rpt. of *College English* 47.6 (1985): 594–607.

Scott, Fred Newton. Preface. *Thomas De Quincey: Essays on Style, Rhetoric, and Language*. Ed. Fred N. Scott. Boston: Allyn, 1893. iii–v. Print.

Secor, Marie. "The Legacy of Nineteenth-Century Style Theory." *Rhetoric Society Quarterly* 12.2 (1982): 76–94. Print.

Shaftesbury, Anthony Ashley Cooper, Third Earl of. Sensus Communis: *An Essay on the Freedom of Wit and Humour*. Treatise II, *Characteristicks of Men, Manners, Opinions, and Times*. Vol. 1. 1711. Indianapolis: Liberty Fund, 2001. 39–93. Print. 3 vols.

Sherry, Richard. *A Treatise of Schemes and Tropes*. 1550. Ed. and introduction by Herbert W. Hildebrandt. Gainesville: Scholars', 1961. Print.

Smith, Adam. *Lectures on Rhetoric and Belles Lettres Delivered in the University of Glasgow by Adam Smith Reported by a Student in 1762–63*. Ed. John M. Lothian. Carbondale: Southern Illinois UP, 1971. Print. Landmarks in Rhetoric and Public Address Series. General ed. David Potter.

———. *The Theory of Moral Sentiments*. 1759. Ed. Knud Haakonssen. Cambridge: Cambridge UP, 2002. Print. Cambridge Texts in the History of Philosophy Series. Ed. Karl Ameriks and Desmond M. Clarke.

Smith, Julianne. "Private Practice: Thomas De Quincey, Margaret Oliphant, and the Construction of Women's Rhetoric in the Victorian Periodical Press." *Rhetoric Review* 23.1 (2004): 40–56. Print.

Snyder, Robert Lance. Editor's introduction. Snyder, *Thomas De Quincey*, xvii–xxiv.

———, ed. *Thomas De Quincey Bicentenary Studies*. Norman: U of Oklahoma P, 1985. Print.

Struever, Nancy S. "The Conversable World: Eighteenth-Century Transformations of the Relation of Rhetoric and Truth." Bialostosky and Needham, *Rhetorical Traditions* 233–49.

Talley, Paul M. "De Quincey on Persuasion, Invention, and Style." *Central States Speech Journal* 16.4 (1965): 243–54. Print.

Thron, E. Michael. "Thomas De Quincey and the Fall of Literature." Snyder, *Thomas De Quincey* 3–19.

Ulman, H. Lewis. *Things, Thoughts, Words, and Actions: The Problem of Language in Late-Eighteenth-Century British Rhetorical Theory*. Carbondale: Southern Illinois UP, 1994. Print.

Veeder, Rex. "Expressive Rhetoric, a Genealogy of Ideas, and a Case for the British Romantics." *Rhetoric, Cultural Studies, and Literacy: Selected Papers from the 1994 Conference of the Rhetoric Society of America*. Ed. John Frederick Reynolds. Hillsdale: Erlbaum, 1995. 99–107. Print.

———. "Romantic Rhetoric and the Rhetorical Tradition." *Rhetoric Review* 15.2 (1997): 300–320. Print.

Walzer, Arthur E. "Aristotle's Rhetoric, Dialogism, and Contemporary Research in Composition." *Rhetoric Review* 16.1 (1997): 45–57. Print.

Warner, Michael. *The Letters of the Republic: Publication and the Public Sphere in Eighteenth-Century America*. Cambridge: Harvard UP, 1990. Print.

Wellek, Rene. "De Quincey's Status in the History of Ideas." *Philological Quarterly* 23.3 (1944): 248–72. Print.

Whale, John C. "'In a Stranger's Ear': De Quincey's Polite Magazine Context." Snyder, *Thomas De Quincey* 35–53.

Whately, Richard. *Elements of Rhetoric*. 1828. New York: Sheldon, 1871. Print.

Williams, Raymond. *Culture and Society: 1780–1950*. New York: Columbia UP, 1983. Print.

Wilson, Thomas. *Arte of Rhetorique*. 1553. Ed. G. H. Mair. Oxford: Clarendon, 1908. Print.

Wordsworth, William. Preface to the *Lyrical Ballads*. 1802. *Lyrical Ballads, by William Wordsworth and Samuel Taylor Coleridge*. 2nd ed. Ed. Michael Mason. Harlow: Pearson, 2007. 55–87. Print.

Zappen, James P. *The Rebirth of Dialogue: Bakhtin, Socrates, and the Rhetorical Tradition*. Albany: State U of New York P, 2004. Print.

Index

Lois Peters Agnew is an associate professor at Syracuse University, where she teaches courses in writing and rhetorical history and theory. Her previous publications include *Outward, Visible Propriety: Stoic Philosophy and Eighteenth-Century British Rhetorics* and articles in journals such as *College Composition and Communication*, *Rhetorica*, *Rhetoric Review*, and *Rhetoric Society Quarterly*.